P+W

$7.50

11 LB

m

D1596954

Invasion Road

Invasion Road

Philip Warner

CASSELL
LONDON

Cassell Ltd.
35 Red Lion Square, London WC1R 4SG
and at Sydney, Auckland, Toronto, Johannesburg,
an affiliate of
Macmillan Publishing Co., Inc.,
New York.

First published 1980

ISBN 0 304 30543 X

Typeset by Inforum Ltd., Portsmouth
Printed in Hong Kong

Contents

Illustrations

Introduction

Invasions are as old as the history of mankind. In the following pages we look at the motives, methods, problems and defences against invasions, of which, of course, there are many different kinds. This takes us back into prehistoric times and up to the present day; it also implies it would be wise to consider the possibilities of the future.

A detailed study is made of Britain as an object of invasion. There is a widespread belief that there have only been two invasion attempts on Britain, the Roman and the Norman, both of which were successful. In fact there have been many planned, and there have been a number of raids which if continued could have been very dangerous indeed. There were times of great peril and urgency in the Napoleonic Wars and again in 1940, both of which are examined in detail. An invasion usually involves the occupation of land but some invasions have begun with penetration of nations by ideas, influences, propaganda, finance, before or even without any movement of troops. In 1940 France was invaded physically but the process of German penetration had been begun long before, and sapped French will to resist. Most people feel that American cultural penetration is benign (although extremely effective through films, radio and selling) but there are countries which hate and resent the 'invasion' of American finance and thought. There are people in Britain who express such anti-American views but most of them seem oblivious to political penetration from other sources.

Those who study the past and ponder the future will appreciate the words 'the price of peace is eternal vigilance'.

But the defences which served so well in the past may not be so effective — even if available — against modern dangers. If Britain is to survive as an independent country it is essential to learn from the past and provide for the future.

1 Why Invade?

Today the thought of the British Isles being invaded seems — to most people — so improbable as to be almost ludicrous. It is not quite so remote from the minds of NATO planners who staged an exercise in the Shetlands in 1978 in order to assess such a possibility. Nor perhaps is it entirely removed from the minds of potential enemies.

There are plenty of people alive today who recall the shock of realizing in 1940 that the Nazi stormtroopers were not at a safe distance behind the allegedly uncrossable Maginot Line but, instead, poised ready to land on these shores. In the event, because the Royal Air Force won the Battle of Britain, and proved decisively to the Germans that they had not the air superiority necessary to cover an invasion, the crisis passed. After the development of tactical nuclear weapons in the post-war era it was smugly assumed by many that an invasion of Britain could no longer take place because the concentration of troops required for an invasion would produce the perfect nuclear target. More nonsense has been talked about the possibilities of nuclear weapons than about almost any other device in the history of warfare. The factors governing their use will be discussed later in this book; for the time being it may be said that nuclear weapons have merely caused a change in the tactics of invasion, not the strategy.

Every would-be invader begins with an assessment of the possible losses and gains. An invader, particularly one who has to cross water or mountains, takes an enormous risk. If he is repulsed, his invasion force will almost certainly be destroyed. He will ask himself whether such a confrontation is necessary.

The D-Day invasion and the earlier invasions of Italy and Sicily were a nicely calculated risk; the Italian invasion of Greece earlier in the war was an example of ruinous miscalculation.

Throughout history there have been many projected invasions of this country but only two have been successful. It should be remembered, however, that there have been a number of occasions when small numbers of enemy troops have been able to land in this country and conduct damaging raids. Some of these raids, in pre-Norman times, led to settlement and partial conquest. How many raiding parties — one might conjecture in the 1980s — does one need to achieve the objective of full-scale invasion?

There are, it seems, many forms of invasion and there are many different motives behind them. The best known of recent invasions are those of Hungary in 1956 with tanks, and of Suez in the same year by airborne forces. These attracted much adverse publicity — a fact which was ignored by the Russians but treated with great seriousness by the Western world. Subsequently there have been less publicized but none the less effective invasions. An interesting contrast was provided by the situation in Angola in 1975. South African troops entered the country and were within an ace of achieving their objective when criticism from the USA caused them to lose confidence in their role. It was otherwise with the Cubans who were able to achieve all their objectives with Russian support. In view of the fact that America has come in for heavy criticism both over Angola and the Suez crisis, it should be remembered that Americans for the most part believe that other countries should settle their own internal affairs. This view was reinforced by the disaster of Vietnam, and persists in spite of President Carter's intervention in the Arab–Israeli dispute and his pronouncements on such matters as human rights behind the Iron Curtain. American politicians have recently expressed views on the internal affairs of Zimbabwe-Rhodesia and Northern Ireland, but have stopped short at wishing to become involved. Russia, of course, has no such inhibitions. The Russian motive in supporting revolutionary or interventionist movements in other countries is to extend the Russian sphere of influence. It is not, of course, merely to spread

Communism, for Russia regards non-Russian Communism (i.e. that of China or Yugoslavia) with even greater dislike than she does capitalism.

However, there are, as we said earlier, many forms of invasion. An invasion may be precipitated by what seems intolerable provocation. In the Arab–Israeli conflicts Israel's Arab neighbours have generally felt that they were intolerably provoked by the mere presence of the state of Israel on what they considered was Arab soil. The Israelis, on the other hand, felt they were forced to attack to check the harassment they suffered from shelling or raids.

Although to many people invasion may seem to be events of the distant past, it is a sad fact that the threat of invasion is as alive today as ever it was. Few countries in the world can consider themselves immune from some form of invasion. All the countries of western Europe feel apprehension about the massive build-up of the Warsaw Pact countries. The Chinese and — to a lesser extent — the Japanese are well aware of the vast Russian army and navy which could function against them. At the moment of writing (September 1978) the Japanese have just delivered a vast floating dock to the Russians for use at Vladivostok. It will enable the Russians to station aircraft carriers and support vessels at that vital port, and therefore greatly increase Russian strength in the Pacific. Further south, Vietnam has just concluded a successful invasion of Cambodia. Both are Communist totalitarian states — Vietnam is backed by Russia, Cambodia by China.

Africa is already invaded by 40,000 Russian-supplied Cubans and there are guerrilla invasion units operating in Mozambique and Zambia; Rhodesia is constantly invaded and at intervals retaliates. South Africa observes these activities and remains watchful. Central and South America provide two areas in which British action may be required. Guatemala has laid claims to Honduras and the Argentine demands sovereignty over the Falkland Islands.

This is by no means a full account of the invasions and attempts at invasion in recent years but it is enough for the purposes of making a general assessment. What are all these invasions trying to achieve? What, if anything, do they have in common? How far are the purposes likely to be fulfilled?

Invasion, as we have noted, is an extreme step. It can be more destructive to the invading force than to the invaded country. There are hazards which neither side can calculate. When Germany invaded Russia in 1941 who would have predicted that the Russian winter could handicap a modern army just as effectively as it had handicapped the army of Napoleon in 1812? What pessimist would have been believed if he had forecast the June weather conditions in 1944 — with a storm powerful enough to destroy a mobile harbour? Invasion, under any circumstances, is something of a gamble.

But the leaders of modern states are not by nature gamblers. They are usually men who have reached the top by endless perseverance and patience. They are skilled planners, who are already on a pinnacle of success. Why stake everything on a gamble?

The answer is that the decision may not be entirely their own. Some people believe that the Russians have sufficient tanks, missiles and aircraft to invade Western Europe and reach the Channel Ports within days. However, military strategists close to the Kremlin may believe, as many military strategists do, that more resources and more reserves are needed. The great fear of all military nations is that, unless they are constantly modernizing and replacing, their equipment will become out of date. The fact that there are enough nuclear weapons in existence to kill every inhabitant of this planet at least seven times has little influence on the minds of some military strategists who would not consider themselves adequately armed even if every soldier was carrying a nuclear pistol. For many years it was said that the Russians were building up vast armaments because they were terrified of being invaded. It is highly unlikely that this is still their motive. Their armament is maintained at an enormously high level because they find that it gives them influence, self-confidence, and the ability to dispose of surplus production to naïve, potentially friendly countries. Few are the countries which do not have experience of MiG fighters, T34 tanks, AK47 rifles, and Russian surface–to–air missiles.

However hawk-like Russian military advisers may be, two thoughts give them pause. Russia relies heavily on Western capitalism for many vital products: if Russian armies swept over Europe the Russian economy — already in a parlous state — would be likely to collapse and lead to yet another internal revolution. Secondly, the Russian soldier cannot be trusted once he has crossed the frontier. The Russian army musters under two million men and if the Russians decided to use all or part of it as an invasion force it would be very thinly spread among a population of 250 million Europeans. There is a limit to an area of control. The Germans reached it in 1942. It has been said that if the Germans had not been thinking of the effects on public opinion in England and the United States, they would have been far more ruthless and brutal in occupied Europe. Scenes like Oradour would have been the rule, not the exception, if England had been successfully invaded. It is a doubtful claim. The experience of history has shown that if a conqueror is utterly ruthless his policy is counter-productive. Instead of cowing everyone into submission he produces pockets of suicidal resistance which, as they increase in number, deplete and destroy the forces of the conqueror.

So what might make the Russians take the decision to invade? The answer is probably the same as with many other modern invasions. If internal problems became too great for economic or political reasons (human rights agitation), the Russians might take the desperate step of crossing frontiers in order to give their people something else to think about. At the moment the Russian people are encouraged to believe they are threatened by the West. The imagined threat seems greater than their present deprivation and discomfort. Ideologically, the thought that Russia has a controlled press, restricts tourists and its own nationals abroad, and generally deprives the people of 'human' rights is anathema to the West. However, Western politicians are for the most part well aware that, while Russia is ruled by the Kremlin oligarchy, peace is more likely while control is tight than it would be if that control should willingly — or unwillingly — be released.

Thus any Russian invasion would be caused by fear of internal change. China is a threat to Russia because China represents an alternative form of Communism. China challenges for the leadership of world Communism. China might have to be invaded — but only if victory could be swift. The mere size of China, its numbers, and diversity, makes the chance of Russia achieving a successful invasion extremely remote.

Curiously enough, the reason which makes modern 'democratic' republics (usually controlled by a dictator) invade is precisely the same as that which influenced Fascist dictators to do the same earlier in this century. In the 1930s Hitler reiterated a farce of pretending that neighbouring countries were a threat to Germany. The 'threat' was expressed by their ill-treatment of minority groups within their own borders. These minority groups of Germans had been created by the ill-conceived and inefficient Treaty of Versailles. It could almost seem reasonable to assume that if a country persecuted a minority group from another country that was tantamount to threatening the mother country.

Mussolini applied the same formula to the countries he coveted, but his most cynical piece of invasion philosophy was the invasion of Abyssinia in 1935. He claimed bombastically that the Mediterranean was 'Mare Nostrum' ('Our Sea' — the old Roman name for it), and was bankrupting the economy to build up an army, navy and air force simultaneously. Now he had to show results. Accordingly he chose a country which would be ill-armed and without friends. Abyssinia was the perfect target. Mussolini's prestige survived until his disastrous attempt to invade Greece in 1941, but when Italy itself was invaded in 1943 not even his German ally could save him.

All these are or were modern motives for invasion. In earlier centuries the reasons were more varied and complex.

Britain, in prehistoric times, was invaded on many occasions. In the dawn of history tribes wandered aimlessly through the temperate zones. The Palaeolithic Period (the Old Stone Age), lasted from 500,000 BC to 9000 BC. We identify it by the weapons and tools which were used in that period, although as far as we know weapons were used only for killing animals, not for dominating fellow humans. A family probably did not travel very fast or far in a man's lifetime, perhaps a hundred miles was the maximum. But in 400,000 years even the slowest moving groups would cover long distances. All the early peoples were wanderers, so some may have crossed and recrossed the continent several times. In the Old Stone Age nomads came from northern Europe and Scandinavia, crossed the Channel, and settled here. They were the first invaders. They were wanderers who moved to fresh hunting and grazing lands.

In the Mesolithic Period (Middle Stone Age), 9000–4000 BC, invaders came here from northern Africa. Five thousand years seems a comparatively short time in pre-history but it is two and a half times as long as the period which has elapsed since the Romans came here.

Invasions became more frequent in the Neolithic (New Stone Age) period, which lasted from 4000 BC to 1500 BC. These waves of invaders came from the Eastern Mediterranean. They left more traces in this country than their predecessors had done, for we can still see the causewayed camps where they kept their animals. They are usually on hilltops, and have two or three rows of ditches. The causeways are the broad platforms leading to the interiors. Such constructions would have been too vulnerable to be used against anything but animals.

The New Stone Age people brought more than plans for camps. They built long barrows and gallery graves. They also built the vast, mysterious Silbury Hill mound near Marlborough, Wiltshire. It is 130 feet high and 120 feet wide. Nobody knows how or why it was built. They also left henges, stone circles of which the most famous is Stonehenge. They were not as primitive as legend would have us believe: Stonehenge was a feat of mathematics as well as muscle and we know that its builders wove woollen clothes, used shapely drinking vessels, and even successfully practised brain surgery. There is a strong probability that the builders of Stonehenge came from Greece.

These early invaders were long thought to have been of peaceable disposition, but recent evidence shows otherwise. In 1977 excavations at Crickley Hill, near Cheltenham, revealed a Neolithic camp which was defended by a rampart and a ditch. The site provided evidence that it had been attacked, captured, and burnt. The principal weapons of the attackers seem to have been bows and arrows. Over two hundred arrowheads were found on the site. Radio carbon dating placed the battle at approximately 3000 BC. Discovery of this fortification was accidental for the 200 yards of the Neolithic rampart were enclosed within an Iron Age fort constructed some 2,500 years later.

But this battle probably had little to do with invasion. It is more likely to have been conflict arising from local rivalry. On the coast there would have been nothing to oppose invaders and they were probably welcomed by the peoples already here. This period of history may seem impossibly remote to many living today. However, it is with us, not merely in the monuments and excavations they made but in ourselves, in our physical characteristics. This is something particularly noticeable in Wales where physical characteristics are less blended and muted.

The next phase in our early history, the Bronze Age, from 1600–700 BC, brought in a very well-organized community. It had important chieftains who were buried in ornate graves, with the graves of lesser chiefs around them; it used battle-axes, gold, amber, arrows and sharp knives. The dead were buried in round barrows, as may be seen on Salisbury Plain, and the bones show that they were undoubtedly the ancestors of the peoples of South Wales: craftsmen with an eye for beauty, industrious, very dangerous militarily if stirred.

After 700 BC the Bronze Age gave way to the Iron Age, possibly because the iron weapons were more plentiful than their predecessors. In the Iron Age great hill forts were built. Looking over a fort like Maiden Castle, just south of Dorchester, or Cissbury in Sussex gives a totally different conception of the abilities of our ancestors. Perhaps the most surprising facet of such vast earthworks is that they were built with primitive tools. Today we only see the bare outline after 2,000 years of weathering and all the superstructure has gone, but that is impressive enough. There were over two thousand Iron Age forts in Britain, situated from the south coast up to Scotland. Some used as many as ten thousand tree trunks on the ramparts, and involved cutting fifty thousand tons of chalk — probably one of the most difficult substances to excavate with primitive tools. We suspect that the Celt played a leading part in the invasion warfare of this era. The Celt is tall, fair-haired, and aggressive. Among the later Celtic invaders were the Marnians, so named because they had previously lived around the River Marne in France. They brought in what was called 'La Tène' culture. They covered their helmets, swords and shields with intricate decoration, much like the scroll and rosette engraving on a modern shotgun. They cherished their weapons. They became expert in the use of chariots in warfare. Women had equal status with men and sometimes became chiefs and led their armies into battle.

In the period just before the Romans came to Britain (their first reconnaissance was 55 BC; their first invasion proper in AD 43), there were several waves of invaders. It seems unlikely that these were opposed on the shore but it seems highly probable that they encountered opposition further in. The Belgae were a mixture of Celt and Teuton; they had already given the Romans much trouble and it is possible that the Romans invaded Britain to make sure that the Belgae did not continue to use it as a springboard for further nuisance. One of the Belgae tribes was the Catevellauni, who were experts with the sling. Recently archaeologists found a dump of twenty thousand slingstones at Maiden Castle, Dorset. The Celts also brought religion on to the battlefield. Their priests, men and women, would make themselves horrible and terrifying to look at and dance and curse before the invaders. They frightened the Romans who went to great lengths to catch and kill as many Druid priests as they could. But they did not kill them all and local resistance was stimulated by these dangerous and mysterious opponents. Of all resistance groups, those inspired by religious fanaticism are the most persistent. Politics can make people determined but religion, which offers eternal salvation, can drive people to almost unimaginable feats of endurance and courage.

Among the later Celts came the Brigantes. These warlike people eventually found their way to Yorkshire, from where they moved to Wales. The Romans never effectively subdued them, either by arms or blandishment, although they tried both often enough.

These early invaders all came here because they were basically nomads. Nomads wander because it is their habit but even nomads settle when the onward path is blocked and when conditions seem to suit them. Wanderers who arrived in Britain realized that they had reached the end of the road. The sea lay behind and sea and mountains lay ahead. The lands of

what are now Kent, Sussex, Hampshire and Wiltshire offered
a reasonable living and the climate was no worse than it had
been elsewhere in Europe. Thus they settled. There was no
reason to invade anywhere else nor anywhere else to invade,
unless they found a way to Ireland or to the other side of the
Welsh mountains.

2 Britain on the Defensive

When Julius Caesar brought two legions to Britain in 55 BC he was not making a true invasion, although his force of over 10,000 could scarcely be described as a raiding party. Several thoughts must have been in his mind. Across the Channel was a potentially rich country; traders had already established the fact that there was gold, tin, and products of rich craftsmanship in these islands but the same traders had probably given his intelligence officers less pleasing information. Although some of the Britons were savages who had changed little since the Old Stone Age, there were others who were civilized and well skilled in martial arts. His first landing was at Walmer and it was opposed but not very effectively. His arrival with a large force surprised the peoples of southern Britain but they quickly rallied together, forgetting their differences, and made his progress hard. The country was difficult terrain for an invader. The hill-tops and look-out points all carried fortifications which the Britons occupied when necessary. There were long stretches of impassable fen. Rivers were not confined within banks, as today, but meandered broadly over the lower valleys, in a tangle of trees and closely packed vegetation. The bottoms of the river valleys were nearly as bad as tropical jungle in the rain belts. There were few tracks on the high ground and it was easy for those who knew these to ambush the unwelcome stranger. But the Romans were used to difficulties and they fought their way from point to point, giving a few military lessons as they went, and perhaps learning a few more. The landing had been made late in the year — 23rd August — and Caesar decided to return before the

autumn winds made his passage too difficult. He had no wish
to lose ships; they were some of his most valuable assets.

The following year he made a more thorough attempt. This
time he took five legions and some auxiliaries. This was over
30,000 men but when he came to Dover — news of his arrival
had travelled before him — he found the beaches crowded
with defenders. The advantage of naval supremacy is that you
can pick your landing point so, as before, Caesar rowed past
Dover and landed at Sandwich. He pushed quickly inland but
met opposition on the Stour and Medway. Hardly were all the
legions ashore when a violent storm wrecked their transports.
Caesar's position was now highly vulnerable. He dared not
spare transport to go back for reinforcements or supplies. His
large army would have to live off the country and maintain its
morale in spite of being harassed by the redoubtable Catevellauni. Caesar decided to stake everything on a swift stroke
at his opponents' headquarters, at Wheathampstead in Hert-
fordshire. He reached it and won a decisive battle but his wily
opponent, the indomitable Cassivellaunus, broke out and
directed his efforts at harassing the Romans' long overstretched line of communication. Caesar withdrew with honour, with a few hostages and some promises of tribute from
minor chiefs. His two forays would have confirmed his opinion that Britain would be a difficult land to conquer and that
involvement there might stretch the Roman commitment too
far. There was plenty of trouble already within the boundaries
of the Roman Empire and Caesar was a good enough strategist
to see that pushing the frontiers further outwards might lead
to weakness rather than greater strength. Other conquerors
have had less foresight.

But these abortive reconnaissances led to stronger trade
links between Rome and Britain. Some of the southern chieftains who were harassed by their less civilized neighbours
requested help from Rome to keep their enemies at bay. They
even visited Rome to ask for help, but it was firmly refused.
Then after the death of the British king Cunobelinus (Cym-
beline) who had kept the minor chiefs in order, chaos came
again. This time a petition to the Emperor Claudius made him
decide to conquer Britain once and for all. In AD 43 he sent
Aulus Plautius with four legions and many auxiliaries, prob-

Roman Invasions of Britain

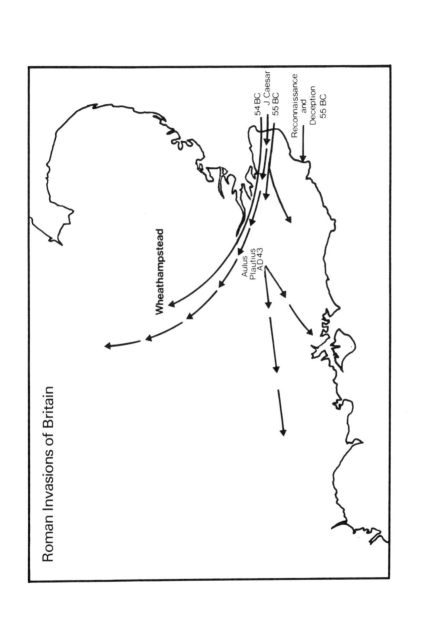

54 BC

J Caesar
55 BC

Reconnaissance
and
Deception
55 BC

Aulus
Plautius
AD 43

Wheathampstead

ably 25,000 men; this was nearly three times as many as William the Conqueror brought when he arrived a thousand years later. Aulus sailed towards Dover, where he was expected, but then turned north and landed at Richborough, Kent. This became his base, and it was fortified as such. Reinforcements then built up his army to 40,000. Unfortunately for Britain the chaos and tribal jealousy which followed Cunobelinus' death made most of the country an easy conquest. But there were centres of resistance. Claudius even thought it worth joining in himself and arrived with elephants; they were probably none the better for their cross-Channel journey. Using ships to good advantage the Romans made a series of landings along the coasts, marched swiftly inland and caught their opponents in the rear. Their toughest battles were around the hill forts. At Worlebury on the Bristol Channel eighteen skeletons show the signs of a desperate last-ditch stand, a garrison dying to a man. At Maiden Castle there were twenty-eight. Some of the latter were women, perhaps Druid priestesses. The numbers may seem small in view of the numbers involved but it should be remembered that most of the bodies would have been dragged away by wild animals, lookers-on, or even surviving relatives. The people in the last ditch would be buried where they fell, crudely and without ceremony. At Spettisbury, near Blandford, there were ninety skeletons, which probably signified it was the last refuge of a tribe which fought to a finish.

Although the Romans occupied Britain and stayed here for four hundred years they never completed the entire conquest of the islands. Wales was a continuing problem, and although they made some headway in the south, the north of Wales, with its mountain fastnesses, could only be isolated, not conquered. The invasions of Scotland were even less successful. The Romans won a bloody battle at Mons Graupius (a site which has never been identified) but soon fell back and tried to keep the Scots from counter-invasion by defensive lines. The Antonine Line and Hadrian's Wall show how seriously the Romans regarded this problem.

When the Romans finally withdrew in the fifth century Britain was already experiencing other invaders. Some of them were Jutes, who settled in Kent, allegedly by invitation.

The Britons, who had forgotten how to defend themselves during the long period of Roman protection hoped that the Jutes would protect them from other seaborne raiders. The Jutes did no such thing. In despair the Britons turned to the Angles, who proved even less satisfactory. They occupied vast tracks of eastern England which became known as East Anglia; there were two main groups: the North Folk and the South Folk. Meanwhile the Saxons continued to drift in. The Britons tried to oppose them on the south coast but made the mistake of trying to defend the old Roman fort at Pevensey. The Saxons besieged it and the Britons were massacred. One of the Saxon chiefs, Wlencing, settled in what is now known as Lancing, another, Cissa, gave his name to Chichester.

These new invaders founded various kingdoms. The South Saxon kingdom became Sussex, the East Saxon kingdom became Essex, the Middle Saxons (in what is now London) became Middlesex and the West Saxons, perhaps the most powerful of all, became Wessex. Wessex extended all over Hampshire, Dorset and Wiltshire; soon it would reach to the Bristol Channel. Surrey hardly existed; it was merely South Rige, the name given to the ridge of high ground to the south of the Thames.

For many years it has been believed that the chain of Roman forts from Brancaster in Norfolk to Portchester in Hampshire was built by the Romans to deter the Saxon invaders. Anderida, now called Pevensey (Sussex), was usually the headquarters of the Roman official responsible for the defence of the Channel approaches. He was known as the Count of the Saxon Shore. The Romans had a useful fleet and their counter-invasion technique was to intercept and destroy the raiders at sea. To a Roman a fortress was never a refuge except in an unexpected disaster — the normal pattern was a fort with broad gateways from which the legionaries could emerge rapidly and without hindrance. Thus their shore forts were for mobile fleets not static defence.

However the vast strength of Portchester and Pevensey seem so greatly in excess of what was needed to repel Saxon raiders that some other explanation is needed. It is suggested that they were constructed for use *against Romans* by Carausius, a Count of the Saxon Shore, when in the year 286 he decided to become an independent Roman emperor. The Roman Empire was ruled jointly by Diocletian and Maximian at this time but Carausius thought he was a match for the pair of them. His little empire consisted of Britain and part of the French coast. He reigned for seven years, striking coins which bear his name. However, he was always aware that his rival emperors might well decide to send a fleet against him, and he strengthened his shore forts accordingly; he built a similar chain of defence along the French coast. Attempts were made to surprise Carausius but the Channel weather and Carausius' naval skill seem to have caused them to be abandoned, and Rome reluctantly recognized the de facto supremacy of the usurper emperor. After a reign of seven years Carausius was murdered by Allectus, his Chancellor of the Exchequer. (It is noteworthy that Chancellors no longer murder their enemies but merely strangle them to death with taxation.) Allectus then became the next British emperor but three years later he was defeated by an army which invaded by creeping ashore under cover of fog. By the time Allectus realized they were ashore they were behind him. In the nineteenth century the Palmerston forts around Portsmouth were built to protect the naval base against a similar type of surprise — from inland.

Looking at the great bastion towers at Portchester with their mountings for heavy catapults which were a very effective form of shore battery it is clear that they were planned for larger and heavier ships than those of the Saxons. But like many other magnificent fortifications they were never used for the purpose for which they were originally built.

The invasions in the south of England were by no means the only incursions Britain suffered in the next thousand years. In the north and even along the west coast of Wales there were descents by marauding Norsemen, who, driven from their own bare country by land hunger, decided to settle in this country. Above all invaders they exploited the military principles of surprise, concentration of force, and flexibility. In their fast manoeuvrable boats they could cover up to 150 miles in a day, descend out of the morning mists, capture the nearest horses and, having become cavalry, raid far inland. Then, loaded with plunder, they re-embarked, perhaps to land again further along the coast. Sometimes they sailed their shallow-draught boats up the winding rivers and creeks, the 'wiks'; this may have been the origin of the word Viking. Whether called Vikings or Norsemen or Danes they were dreaded by all. Terror was their message. A party of twenty or thirty could make a series of successive strikes and thus appear to be a force of several hundred. 'From the fury of the Norsemen,' went up the prayer, 'Good Lord, deliver us.' Those who became early settlers soon found themselves having to devise a form of defence against later arrivals. It usually consisted of a form of ambush but had to be preceded by an efficient signal warning system enabling a local community to take refuge in a 'burh'. A burh was an enclosure, not usually on a hill-top like the Iron Age forts, but in a cultivated area. It consisted of a ditch or two and thorn palisades. It would be just strong enough to need more time than the invaders could spare to destroy it, and thus they left the burhs alone. Later, many of the burhs became permanent settlements — 'burghs' or little townships. Edinburgh was Edwin's burgh, but not all former 'burghs' incorporate the Saxon word. Tamworth (in Staffordshire) was a burgh, and a centre of resistance, but the name does not disclose the fact.

Thus land hunger drove in the Vikings to try to dispossess the Angles and Saxons and Jutes who had come to Britain for the same reason centuries earlier. These were not so much invasions as incursions, but the end result was the same. By the beginning of the eleventh century Britain had a well-defined, organized society. And in the year 1066 the King of England, de facto rather than de jure, was the lively, alert Harold, a small man but a great fighter. He had followed a series of ineffective kings, and before being elected he had shown that he was capable of beating the Welsh raiders in their own country by their own methods and establishing a stable, just government throughout Britain.

Unluckily for Harold, two powerful opponents had envious eyes fixed on this country. One was King Hardrada of Norway described, perhaps accurately, as 'the greatest Viking of them all'. Hardrada had ambitions about conquering Britain and they were stimulated when Harold exiled his own younger brother, Tostig, who was ruling his earldom of

Northumbria harshly and unjustly. Tostig proceeded to Norway, burning with hate and desire for revenge. In consequence, in September 1066, with a fleet of some 300 ships crammed with experienced and bloodthirsty Norwegian warriors, Hardrada and Tostig landed in Yorkshire. Harold, hearing the news, promptly set off to teach both a lesson. So well did he teach it at Stamford Bridge, near York, that the invasion fleet needed a mere twenty-four ships to carry away the remnants of the vast armada which had come in earlier. But while celebrating the victory at York Harold received other news. It is unlikely that he thought it was bad news, for Harold enjoyed a fight, even though he might at this moment have appreciated a little more time to re-equip his army. But morale was high. Had they not just defeated the greatest army the great warrior Hardrada could produce? William of Normandy who, Harold was told, had landed on the south coast, must be confident indeed if he thought he could do better than Tostig and Hardrada.

But William, who had one or two tricks up his sleeve, thought he could. His army, by comparison with Harold's, was modern. He had a variety of weapons and tactics. And he had religious conviction. He also had a device for consolidating the victory he planned to win. It was called the motte and bailey castle. Harold had heard of these. There were in fact three in Britain at the time which had been built by Norman favourites of Edward the Confessor. No one realized that they were one of the most effective instruments of conquest and government yet devised, and soon would be everywhere in the land.

Harold came south, though not quite as quickly as he is normally supposed to have done; he could have arrived at Battle, near Hastings, earlier if he had wished. William no doubt thought Harold would come to Hastings itself, where he had made preparations to receive him. But Harold took up position on Senlac Hill, some seven miles away from Hastings along a ridge. There, surrounded by his faithful house-carls with their bright battle-axes, he waited for William.

The ensuing battle lasted all day. It was rare for ancient battles to last as long as that, and it was almost unknown for them to last for more than one day. Even in a one-day battle it

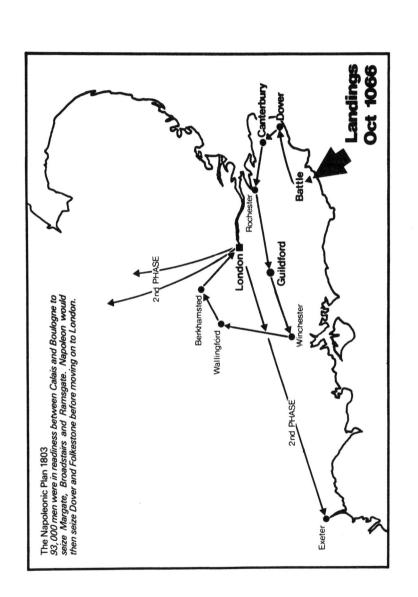

The Napoleonic Plan 1803
93,000 men were in readiness between Calais and Boulogne to seize Margate, Broadstairs and Ramsgate. Napoleon would then seize Dover and Folkestone before moving on to London.

Landings Oct 1066

Canterbury

Dover

Battle

Rochester

London

Guildford

2nd PHASE

Berkhamsted

Wallingford

Winchester

2nd PHASE

Exeter

was impossible to fight continuously. If the sides were evenly matched there would be pauses when men rested their weary arms and legs. It is not possible to swing heavy weapons all day long, or even to shoot arrows for too long a period. Some people find swinging a golf club or tennis racket tiring enough in an hour. They would have fared poorly on a medieval battlefield.

On to the field at Battle William brought cavalry and bowmen. Neither was outstandingly successful. Saxon infantry attacked the horses and brought down the riders. The Norman knights broke up the Saxon formation but in spite of their superior arms and armour took long to push their way forward.

A misunderstanding which caused part of Harold's army to leave their good position enabled the Norman cavalry to make some progress but it was the bowmen who turned an evenly matched struggle into Norman victory. William craftily decided that if the arrows were launched on a high trajectory they would distract the Saxons who were repulsing frontal attacks. But they achieved much more. One chance shot seems to have pierced Harold's unprotected face— it is impossible to know whether it blinded him but the presence of arrows at the vital stage is indicated by the Bayeux tapestry. With their leader fallen the Saxon line was finally broken. An invader who had had the boldness to bring over horses in ships — for horses are extremely poor sailors — and who had waited six weeks for a favourable wind, and had persuaded his followers that God really was on their side, probably deserved to win. It was a pity that he was such an unpleasant character, for the Norman invasion obviously benefited Britain in the long run.

And what was the real reason he came here? Why did he jeopardize his Norman dukedom by invading Britain?

The answer seems to lie in the Norman character. The Normans were the descendants of the Norsemen who had settled in northern France. They liked nothing more than a fight and were restlessly active in many other ways too. William seems to have genuinely believed that he was the true heir to the English throne and was aware that if he won the opening battle he could consolidate his victory. He was accustomed to triumphing over rebuffs. He was the bastard son of a

Norman duke and a tanner's daughter. Of all despised and stinking trades tanning was considered the worst, and William was never very happy about the tannery stigma, but was defiant about being a bastard. Some of his documents began, 'I, William the Bastard . . .' He was a typical Norman. The achievements of this formidable people are astonishing. Not only did they conquer Britain but they also penetrated the Mediterranean and made a durable impact on Sicily and Italy.

By the end of the century in which England had been conquered by the Normans the first of another series of invasions was beginning. These were the Crusades, whose history lies outside our scope, except in one particular. They represented a religious motive for invasion and although the Crusades were inefficient, corrupt and ultimately unsuccessful the concept was ideological. In the Middle Ages men and women would make enormous sacrifices of life, effort, money or time for religious purposes. Religion still motivates many but has now been replaced for the most part by political ideology. In the Middle Ages many forms of cruelty and persecution were practised in the belief that the victims would find salvation that way. Today political systems demand sacrifices and practise tyranny with the bland excuse that they are preparing a better life for future generations. Unfortunately for the victims of religious or political bigotry the value of the benefits they are allegedly receiving from absolutism is not always clear.

The fact that the Normans made French the language of government in Britain, and were themselves of French origin did not prevent a long-lasting hostility developing between the two countries. Invasion of France by England took place on several occasions in the ensuing centuries when English monarchs were trying to prove their right to rule France. Edward III and Henry V made extensive probes into France but ultimately achieved little except temporary glory and more permanent financial instability. Edward I invaded Wales and Scotland as his predecessors had done before him, and as others would do after him. The clashes with Wales and Scotland were in a sense border disputes; there were more serious matters elsewhere. In 1216 the English barons were so irritated by King John that they invited a French army over to help dethrone him. John was an able warrior when he bestirred himself but he died before he could come to grips with this invasion army. However, in the meantime, the French army had besieged and captured several castles in southern England, though failing at others. The Channel was a lawless sea in the Middle Ages and abounded with pirates and smugglers. Like the Scottish border it could see more fighting in times of alleged peace than in declared war. The English raided Sluys in 1297. Portsmouth was raided and burnt by the French in March 1338 and Southampton received the same treatment in October 1338. Southampton was refortified, and beat off a French attack in 1339. In 1416 the French blockaded Portsmouth and sacked Portland; in 1457 four thousand French from Honfleur raided Sandwich and killed the mayor; his successors have worn a black gown in memory ever since. In 1475 there was a French raid on Portland but it was beaten off.

A major crisis occurred when Henry VIII managed to alienate France and Spain simultaneously. During the years from 1531 to 1545 there was constant danger that a combined Franco–Spanish fleet would arrive at the south coast. Strenuous efforts were made to build up a navy, and a chain of impressive artillery forts was begun. Most of them still stand today at places like Deal, Camber, Portland, Walmer, Hurst, and Pendennis, to name but a few. They are open to visitors who marvel to think that such sophistication was present in warfare as long as four hundred years ago. But they did not deter the French who in 1545 sent 225 ships into the Solent and sacked the Isle of Wight.

Just over a hundred years after the French raid on Portland the nation was once more alert with invasion fears. This time it was the Spaniards. Queen Elizabeth had played off the French against the Spanish and vice versa for long enough; clearly someone had to teach England a lesson and Spain, greatly provoked by British maritime activities, was only too glad to undertake the task. Thus the Great Armada came into being.

In 1585 Queen Elizabeth made no secret of the fact that she was sending aid to the Dutch who were bitterly hostile to the Spaniards. The Spanish government was extremely angry and uttered threats and warnings. England stirred herself, but not very much. A warning system was established to call out troops who were not even mobilized. (It was almost like 1939 when there were excellent arrangements for calling out units which existed on paper only.) In 1585 iron baskets on long poles were set up at fifteen-mile intervals. In an emergency they would be ignited; some were — by accident, causing much inconvenience in their area.

The news that the Armada had set sail reached England in July 1588. The militia was called out but it took an average of ten days for the citizen soldiers to take up their defence positions. In theory some 50,000 men were called up; in reality the figures were probably considerably less. In the event the militia was not needed. The Spanish plan was to sail past England to the Netherlands where the fleet would pick up trained soldiers and reinforcements, but, not for the first time, naval plans went awry in the Channel. English ships were small and manoeuvrable. For reasons of economy sailors had to be soldiers when needed and the ships were small because it was not possible to afford the larger craft of Henry VIII's day. These light manoeuvrable craft engaged the cumbersome Spanish galleons in the western approaches and mauled them all the way to Calais, which was an assembly point. As they lay in Calais harbour, Lord Howard sent eight fireships in among them. The resultant chaos did untold harm to Spanish morale which was already low; some ships left harbour only to be wrecked, other Spanish ships, waiting off Gravelines, were caught by English gunfire. The Spanish fleet moved north in considerable disarray only to be put into worse state by a sudden violent storm. The threat of invasion was over and the militia stood down on 19th August.

Today we know that the Spanish Armada of 130 ships, 8,000 sailors and 20,000 soldiers was an indifferent fighting force. We know the commander-in-chief was incompetent and the crews were unused to sailing in the type of waters encountered round these islands. But it did not seem that way to the people of Britain who apprehensively watched from the shore or waited for tidings further inland. It seemed a very formidable force indeed. It is easy to be wise after the event; military history contains many examples of underestimates and over-confidence, or the reverse. The threat of the Armada passed, but it was real enough in the summer of 1588. There were other alarms subsequently which caused the militia to be called out, but fears proved unfounded. The reasons why Spain planned the Great Armada are easy to understand. To Spain, England seemed a treacherous, heretical country which could only be brought to heel by military and naval means. English sailors had a long history of privateering and piracy in Spanish waters. Thus the Spanish belief went. But the English felt they were sturdy Protestants fighting against religious tyranny, and disputed the Spanish claim to ownership of the waters round South America, so grandiloquently termed the 'Spanish Main'.

After the Armada the invasion threat receded for nearly a century. Then it suddenly appeared in a classic case of 'a wrong war at a wrong time'. In the second half of the seventeenth century France was under the domination of the insatiably ambitious Louis XIV. His intention was the conquest of neighbouring Europe. Unfortunately, in 1665, England and Holland were at loggerheads over their rivalry in East Indian trade and war broke out between them. There were two naval battles, the first of which England won but the second was inconclusive, but although honours were even the English fleet had sustained so much damage that it could not hope to put to sea without extensive repair and refit. The money which Parliament granted to Charles II for that purpose was promptly squandered by him on other projects and in 1667 a Dutch fleet was able to sail up the Medway, burn sixteen ships and destroy most of Chatham dockyard. The only satisfactory defence came from a battery hastily installed at Upnor Castle. It was a black day for England but the elusive Charles II, ever intriguing, was able to achieve a satisfactory treaty with the Dutch which even gave England possession of New Amsterdam, later to be called New York. Soon afterwards the countries forgot their differences and combined against the French.

The danger from France, though diminished by Marlborough's victories in Europe, never completely disappeared until the beginning of the present century. It revived in the great wars of the mid-eighteenth century and reached its peak when Napoleon massed 120,000 French troops on the French coast between 1803 and 1805. The threat of invasion seemed very close — even though the British navy had Nelson and

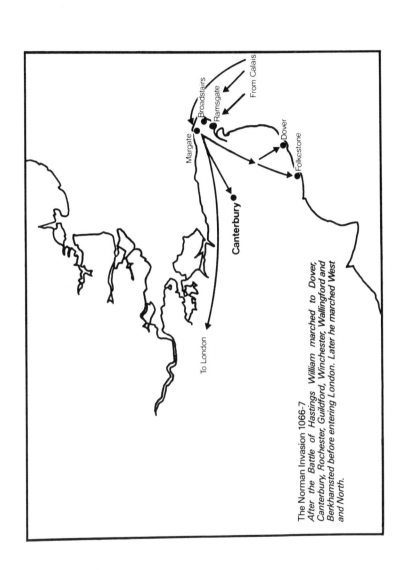

The Norman Invasion 1066-7
After the Battle of Hastings William marched to Dover,
Canterbury, Rochester, Guildford, Winchester, Wallingford and
Berkhamsted before entering London. Later he marched West
and North.

other excellent captains — for stories came across the Channel of the French practising embarking and disembarking with their transports. There has always been a mysterious traffic across the Channel, mainly of smugglers but of spies and agents too. There was a surprising amount of open trading as well. Half a million men stood to on the British coast for two and a quarter years waiting for the invasion that never came.

Napoleon's aim was as clear to others as to himself. At sea the French were constantly frustrated and often blockaded by the British navy. On land British intervention gave aid and courage to opponents whom otherwise Napoleon could have decisively knocked out of his path. The only way a maritime power such as Britain could be destroyed was a successful strike at the centre. That strike could be nothing less than full-scale invasion.

But before Trafalgar gave him a decisive naval defeat Napoleon had decided that the invasion was not feasible. Instead he would amass victories in Europe and, with the Continent in his control, bring Britain to her knees. But his ambitions ended on the island of Elba.

After the tremendous battering sustained in the Napoleonic Wars — which lasted almost continuously from 1793 to 1815 — over twenty years of war — it might have been thought that France's military ambitions would have been adequately blunted and the threat of invasions of Britain would cease. But it was not to be. Throughout the nineteenth century there was a series of invasion scares, particularly during the reign of the Emperor Napoleon III. The first major crisis was in 1844 when a French admiral annexed the island of Tahiti and arrested the British consul. The king of the French at this time was Louis-Philippe. His own throne was unstable and he considered that Britain might be his most reliable ally in Europe. He therefore defused the situation by insisting that his ministers should send a formal apology to Britain and abandon Tahiti. Britain calmed down, but only slowly. In that year frenzied preparations had been made to repel a possible invasion from France. The situation had scarcely cooled when public indignation was ablaze again. In 1846, by a series of crafty marriages, Louis-Philippe managed to put his own younger son in line for the Spanish throne. If there was one alliance the British would not tolerate it was the union of France and Spain under one king. The whole of Marlborough's wars had been fought to prevent just such an eventuality and Sir Robert Peel, leader of the Conservative party, made it very clear that England would not allow such an event. The country began to be put on a war footing, as if there was not enough trouble already from the Chartists and the famine in Ireland. But this invasion crisis passed when Louis-Philippe and his dynastic pretensions were swept away in the Revolution of 1848.

Napoleon III, who was the nephew of Napoleon I, had begun his political career when he had been elected President of the French Republic; although only a year had passed since the 1848 revolution the 'republic' had already become a military dictatorship. In 1851 Napoleon organized a coup d'état, imprisoned his political opponents and made himself emperor. Then he set about looking for military glory appropriate to the nephew of the great, though ultimately unsuccessful, Bonaparte.

The immediate danger of a French invasion of Britain was averted by a Russian invasion of Turkish territories in 1853, which led to the Crimean War, and a consequent Anglo-French invasion of the Crimean Peninsula in the Black Sea. Both these invasions were the result of naked power politics: Russia trying to dismember Turkey and reach the Mediterranean over the pieces and Britain and France trying to prevent this — and succeeding. However, his share in the glory was not enough for Napoleon III.

After the Crimean War was over the French dictator was temporarily at a loss for a suitable place to display his military ambition. He had promised to help the Italians throw off their Austrian overlords but the campaign looked difficult and unrewarding so he had done little but utter vainglorious promises. In 1858 Orsini, an Italian exile who had become disappointed by Napoleon's unfulfilled promises to help his party to Italian independence, decided to murder his bogus benefactor. He therefore threw a bomb at the Emperor's carriage; investigations proved the plot had been conceived, and the bomb made, in London. Although Napoleon and his wife, the Empress Eugénie, escaped, several members of their entourage were killed. Orsini was immediately executed.

To Napoleon and the French this was clearly a hostile act by England. Why shelter such a dangerous revolutionary? The English parliament tried to calm matters by hastily drafting a bill condemning political assassinations whether inside or outside England. But it was not enough for French public opinion which was whipped up by their press. The French army growled and some of its senior officers petitioned the Emperor to allow them to destroy what they described as 'the infamous haunt in which machinations so infernal are hatched'. The effect of this bellicose statement on British public opinion may be imagined. Parliament failed to pass the new bill (known as the Conspiracy to Murder Bill) and Palmerston resigned. His Liberal government was replaced by the Conservatives under Lord Derby and Disraeli. The new administration lasted only a year but in that time brought in the Volunteer Movement which provided a permanent auxiliary force which could be called on to assist the regular army in home defence. The volunteers armed themselves and paid for their own training, but the force was popular and enrolled 170,000 men in the first year. The movement continued even though the French threat abated. In 1859 Napoleon at long last attacked Austria and beat them at Magenta and Solferino. At that point he stopped and, having annexed Nice and Savoy as compensation for his trouble, left the Italians to fend for themselves. This they did very well under the leadership of Garibaldi.

The presence of such an erratic and vainglorious emperor in a neighbouring country was certainly reasonable cause for wary apprehension in Britain. However, across the Channel a brisk smuggling trade still flourished and for many English and French the only enemies were the customs officers. Culturally there were close ties between the two countries and the manoeuvrings of politicians seemed far removed from ordinary life.

There were however real military problems. France possessed more warships than Britain and she had heavy artillery with a range of 8,000 yards. This meant that if a raiding force could succeed in landing with a few guns and could position them on the hills behind Portsmouth the town could be shelled from the rear while the French navy attacked from the sea. The idea that the French might land heavy artillery and drag it up

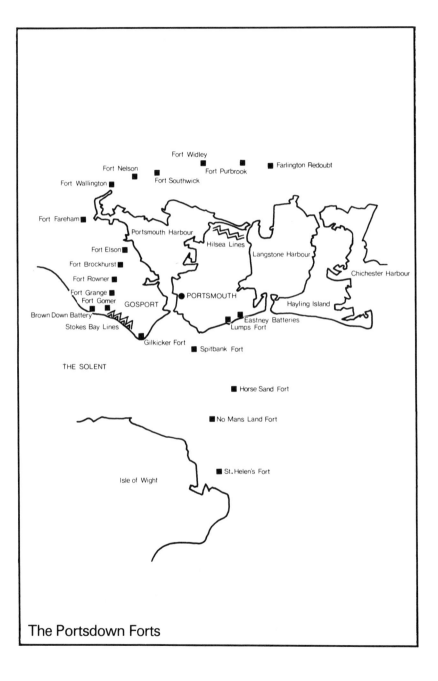

Fort Widley

Fort Nelson

Fort Purbrook

Farlington Redoubt

Fort Southwick

Fort Wallington

Fort Fareham

Portsmouth Harbour

Hilsea Lines

Langstone Harbour

Fort Elson

Chichester Harbour

Fort Brockhurst

Fort Rowner

Fort Grange

PORTSMOUTH

Fort Gomer

Hayling Island

Brown Down Battery

GOSPORT

Stokes Bay Lines

Eastney Batteries

Lumps Fort

Gilkicker Fort

Spitbank Fort

THE SOLENT

Horse Sand Fort

No Mans Land Fort

St. Helen's Fort

Isle of Wight

The Portsdown Forts

the hills to the rear of Portsmouth harbour seems to belong to the strategy of the armchair rather than the operations room. But the decision to build defensive forts there was taken by a Royal Commission set up to 'Consider the Defence of the United Kingdom'. Work began in 1860 and eight years later five Portsdown forts — Purbrook, Widley, Southwick, Nelson and Wallington had all been completed (and irreverently nicknamed 'Palmerston's Follies'). Like many fortifications they were out of date and no longer needed when completed. However, they made excellent shelters in World War II.

The Portsdown forts were by no means the only ones to be built in this period. Alderney, being a mere twenty miles from the French coast, had an extensive range of expensive fortifications which were never completed. Fort Albert could house 2,000 men — enough for almost any contingency.

There were too many political rivalries between France and Britain for them to be anything but watchful neighbours during the nineteenth century. The Germans, who had decisively crushed the French in 1870, then imposed such a heavy indemnity upon them that they assumed that France could not revive for a quarter of a century at least. The French paid off the indemnity at such bewildering speed, and looked so strong again, that the Germans seriously considered attacking them again as a 'security measure'. Britain's reaction to the vigorous military France of the 1880s was to build yet another chain of fortifications. This time it was designed to guard London and consisted of a line of redoubts and storehouses extending along a line running from Guildford through Knockholt into Essex. A surviving fortified storehouse may be seen at Farningham, Kent (near Eynsford). If needed these points were to be manned by volunteers. They were neglected after France and Britain reached a better political understanding at the turn of the century.

But the Anglo-French Entente, directed against the growing power of Imperial Germany, did not remove invasion fears from British minds. The French bogey gave way to the German bogey. In the period up to 1914 invasion scares often fluttered through men's minds, stimulated by a series of interesting books. But the tremor of anticipation was quickly settled by the thought of the new British battleships, the

Dreadnoughts, the first of which had been launched in 1906. They would stop these foreign monkey tricks. 'We want eight and we won't wait' was the rallying cry. And the battleship certainly looked as good a defender of our shores as could be wished. This confidence in vast ironclads was subsequently found to be misplaced but the trust the public had in the navy as a whole was soundly based.

In retrospect it is difficult to believe that any of the nineteenth-century invasion scares were justified. Hard words do not always mean hard blows — at times they are a substitute for them. Certainly if Louis-Philippe or Napoleon III had been asked to find a reason for invading Britain they would have been hard put to find one. They would have been even harder pressed if they had tried to put such plans into execution.

The same remained true of the Germans in World War I. The German High Command had seen adequate reason to invade France, even if it meant violating Belgian neutrality. The German navy could shell ports in this country and German aeroplanes and Zeppelins could bomb inland towns. But to put a landing force ashore would have been an entirely different matter, even if France had capitulated in 1918 in the great spring offensive.

Invasion only became a genuine threat again in 1940. Then indeed the Germans had cause to wish to complete their conquest of Europe. But even without the setback of the Battle of Britain Hitler might have thought very carefully before he launched what must have seemed a potentially long and dangerous campaign. His main objective was to destroy Soviet Russia by reaching into its heartland, to Moscow, to Leningrad, to Stalingrad. By this time he would have acquired vast resources and proclaimed himself to the world as a greater general than Napoleon. There were good reasons for invading Britain if it could be accomplished as quickly and easily as the conquest of France. At the time he did not believe it could be. Radar and British Intelligence had deceived him about the number of British planes and resources. Wherever his bombers went there seemed to be fighters to meet them. He believed that there were twenty-four British divisions operationally ready in southern England. Actually there were four and their operational readiness was not anywhere near as well advanced as their commanders would have wished. Like many other of Britain's enemies Hitler must have asked himself the vital question 'Why Invade?' and been unable to answer it to his own satisfaction.

> He either fears his fate too much
> Or his deserts are small
> Who durst not put it to the touch
> To win or lose it all.

This is a fine rousing little verse but it has no message for would-be invaders. Successful generals only offer battle when they consider their opponents have little chance of winning. Would-be invaders should only move when they are *certain* they will win.

The story of Hitler's invasion plans will be told later and compared with the counter-invasion which came four years later. Four years. That two-word phrase has implications which are usually overlooked. In the minds of many, a war is a transitory matter — for that is how it appears in television, films or books. In reality it is vastly different; it seems endless to those concerned. Yet in comparison with some of the wars of history the six years of World War II or four years of World War I are short indeed. Wars are rarely short, even the Crimean War which many people assume consisted of little but the Charge of the Light Brigade was a slogging two-and-a-half-year struggle. The Napoleonic Wars lasted almost continuously from 1798 to 1815. Marlborough's wars lasted from 1701 to 1709, and the Seven Years War of 1756–63 was only the continuation of a struggle which had been going on since 1739, in fact about a twenty-four-year war.

A curious feature of wars is that much of the necessary provision for them is not made till they are nearly over. Sometimes the preparations, particularly if they are fortifications, are being extended long after the war has finished and danger is already presenting itself from a different area — for which, of course, these preparations are useless. Occasionally, however, a skill, weapon, or fortification from an earlier period may refuse to become obsolete, or may have become discarded, almost forgotten, then revived. Thus in World War II the guerrilla soldier of the early nineteenth century became very useful in behind-the-lines operations; he would have been useless in World War I for there was nowhere for him to exercise his talents. Equally, the Vickers machine-gun, although officially obsolete, was found to be very useful for certain types of fighting in World War II. And in the counter-insurgency warfare of the last thirty years a very useful fortification has been the sangar, a little stone surface shelter of the type which prehistoric man could and did make.

Thus, as Shakespeare put it, 'The whirligig of time brings in his revenges.'

3 'Look to your Moat' — the Story of Coastal Defence

The defence of Britain relies on three processes. The first is the interception of the invaders at sea where they can be attacked by aircraft, submarines, or surface craft; the second is the physical prevention of landing by mining and wiring beaches and establishing strongpoints; the third is the counter-attack which, if a landing is made, will involve those defensive troops not already committed. Should all these fail, protracted intolerable action by resistance groups could theoretically cause the invader to withdraw. In the first century AD the Scots remarked bitterly of the Romans: 'They make a desert and they call it peace.' The Scots then proceeded to make a further desert around the Romans and in consequence the Romans ultimately withdrew to Hadrian's Wall. The science of public relations had not been invented when the Romans invaded Scotland but even if it had been it is doubtful whether the most advanced modern techniques of 'creating a favourable image in a climate of acceptance' would have made much impact on the Scots at that time.

Having asked — and answered — the questions 'Why Invade?' it follows that we should ask the question 'How Invade?' To know how to invade requires a careful study of logistics and intelligence, which we come to later, but the immediate need for a would-be invader is to study the defences likely to be used against him. If we follow their development chronologically we reach a useful understanding of what is effective and what is not. There are still plenty of large-scale anti-invasion defences which can be inspected. Along the north coast of France are the remains of what was once a formidable 'west wall'. Barring entry to East German territory is another formidable wall but this one is designed to keep people in rather than out and is not militarily significant. In the comparatively recent past frontier defences existed to prevent enemies spying on a country's activities. Today no frontier is going to thwart the vision of a spy satellite.

Early shipping seems to have been well in advance of early defences. Boats, at first in the shape of a tree-trunk hollowed out by fire or flints, have existed almost as long as man himself. By the New Stone Age, when Stonehenge was built, there were galleys in existence which could carry men for long distances using a combination of oar and sail. They could also carry heavy weights by an ingenious system of suspending them in the water. Even three thousand years ago there were battle fleets.

The problem of landing on the shores of Britain from the New Stone Age until Roman times was clearly negligible. Invaders could choose a variety of landing points, beach their craft or find an anchorage, and be protected from the occupants by the marshy land between the sea and the uplands. On some shores and lakes, invaders might encounter 'crannogs' which were artificial islands made of logs and stones. A few have survived. They were probably regarded more as refuges than forts, and were far more useful on lakes or rivers than on the coast. A crannog, if defended, could easily block the passage of a river.

But until Roman times it appears that there was little attempt to block invasions on the coast. Instead men retired to the hill forts where they fought on ground of their own choosing. Traditionally at least three men (some say ten) are needed to attack one who is in a prepared defensive position. It may also be better to allow your opponents to land and annihilate them all rather than repel the landing party and then have to deal with other landings elsewhere. In 1944 there was conflict of opinion on the German Staff on this matter. Some thought the Allied invasion force should be repulsed as it attempted to land; others felt it should be resisted but allowed to land and then utterly destroyed, with all its equipment, in a devastating counter-attack.

When the Romans arrived in 55 BC they were met on the

beaches by hostile forces. The ancient Britons had doubtless had news of their coming, and were ready on the shore to meet them, but as yet they were not very well organized. The main resistance was at Dover and each Roman party carefully avoided landing there. However, as ships are slow it was possible for the Britons to prepare a reception wherever the Romans eventually decided to land. But as there were no fixed defences the Romans were able to put their ships into an extended line and infiltrate. The Britons could not cope with the Romans piecemeal, so the latter were able to reach the shore and regroup.

The Romans at first needed no coastal defences. They had command of the sea. Their galleys would have forty oars on each side, in two banks. They also carried a square sail for use when the wind was favourable, but the technique of tacking would remain unknown for over a thousand years. They were about eighty-five feet long and had a high deck on which fighting men could be mustered. The galleys were rowed by their fighting crews, not by slaves. Some carried heavy, stone-throwing ballistas.

In the early stages of the Roman occupation little attention was paid to fixed defences. This is not to say that the Romans did not appreciate the need for these, for when on the march they devoted nearly half the daylight hours to fortifying their camps with ditches and strong points. But there was little fear of attack from the sea.

In the third century AD the Roman Empire was beginning to weaken through corruption and luxury. The virile fighting spirit which had sent its soldiers forcing their way through France, Spain, Germany and Britain seemed spent. It was an inevitable process. Empires have risen through the leadership of dynamic characters and continued as long as national self-confidence produced the will to explore, fight and govern. But when the potential leaders occupy themselves with luxury and the people are infected with lethargy the former empire soon becomes a province of new imperialists.

When the Romans finally withdrew from Britain in the fifth century AD in spite of passionate requests by the Britons for them not to do so, Britain was already experiencing further invasion. The Angles, the Saxons, the Jutes, the Picts, were all marauding and making inroads. Defence was negligible. Sometimes there were local battles which made the invaders consolidate their gains before probing further, but eventually Britain became an Anglo-Saxon kingdom. This is not to say that it was either united or peaceful. Murderous campaigns were fought between rival kings, such as the Mercians and Northumbrians, and the East and West Saxons. Eventually the West Saxons, whose kingdom was known as Wessex and included most of what is now Hampshire, Wiltshire, Dorset and Somerset, became dominant with King Ecgbert who is the direct ancestor of all but three English monarchs and is thus the original member of our present royal line. This was in the early ninth century but even as the Kingdom of Wessex established supremacy there were fresh invaders making their probes. They were Vikings and they were first encountered at Wareham, in Dorset, where they sacked the town. A few years later other bands of these marine predators were plundering towns and monasteries along the northern coastline. Not until 871, when Alfred became King of Wessex, was there a real effort to check them. Alfred lost many battles and had to hide among the crannogs of Somerset before he eventually achieved victory. But it was not by land battles that he planned to cope with future invaders; it was on the sea. For Alfred, rightly, has been called the founder of the English navy.

Unfortunately we do not know the design of Alfred's ships but it seems likely that they were similar to those of the Vikings. They were, however, larger than those of their opponents and this would give them a different appearance. What little we know about them is recorded in meagre entries in the Anglo-Saxon Chronicle. Restored Viking ships may be seen in Norway and there are replicas at Thorpe Water in Surrey and Ramsgate in Kent. Alfred's ships may well have been over two hundred feet long and had some thirty men each side. He encouraged sailors to go on long voyages and successful traders were awarded the rank of thegn. His ships were clinker built — that is, built with the external boards overlapping downward — and had a single mast and a central deck. This deck was some six feet higher than the bottom boards and provided a form of cabin store. However its prin-cipal use was to provide a high platform from which assaults could be launched on to other ships. There is no record of what was contained in this deck area but it seems that it was well used for the shields were outside the central gunwales, not inside as on the Viking ships.

These two types of ship, the Viking *drakkar* and the English trading ship (which could also be quickly adapted to become a warship) were the principal ships seen in Europe during the next two hundred years. When William launched the Norman conquest he assembled a huge army on the French coast at Saint-Valéry, with some four hundred transports to carry it over the Channel. The promise of grants of yet unconquered — even unseen — lands lured an army of some 60,000 — in fact all the adventurers and riff-raff of Europe. Among them was an eighty-year-old French nobleman. However, not all were rogues and robbers; inevitably there were men of honour among them. Less than a quarter of the volunteers were able to sail, for room had to be found on the transports for the horses. The largest craft could transport three hundred men, the smallest thirty or forty. The fleet had been constructed hastily and the standard of seamanship was so low that calm weather was vital. But with Harold occupied in the north the crossing passed without major mishap.

Harold had therefore lost the campaign before a single blow had been struck in the battle of Hastings. During the six months' build-up of William's invasion fleet Harold's ships had patrolled the Channel. A risky attempt to destroy the transports while they lay at anchor had not been attempted; the prevailing winds would have helped the raid but hindered the getaway. But at the critical moment, just before the wind changed, Harold's attention was directed north and he seems to have left no instructions for his navy. Thus a superior army, with better armour and tactics, was able to establish itself on the English mainland.

The lessons of the Norman invasion were not forgotten by those who had taught them and for the next two hundred years the Channel was an Anglo-Norman sea. The only danger came from the Flemish who were a powerful naval force in the twelfth century. English ships ventured far afield. Sailors who had learnt their trade around the coasts of Britain were deterred neither by Atlantic storms nor the squalls and pirates of the Mediterranean. Britain has the greatest length of coastline in proportion to its size of any country in the world. Furthermore that coastline is beset with hazards: the weather in the Channel can be treacherous, the coasts of Cornwall and Wales are surrounded by wrecks, and the sea around Scotland is an area which even the most experienced sailors approach with caution.

Considerable encouragement was given to English shipping by the needs of the Third Crusade, which began in 1190. In the event the Crusader fleet suffered heavy losses from bad weather and had little effect on the campaign. The Crusade itself sowed the seeds of much bitterness between the participating nations, principally England and France. In consequence, when the English barons were trying to remove King John from the English throne, they had no hesitation in asking the French Prince Louis, heir to the French throne, to invade this country and assist them in their rebellion. Louis landed in Kent and marched across the country with varying success. The Cinque Ports refused him entry and he sustained a humiliating setback at Odiham in Hampshire. John, who was in the north, marched south to confront the invader but lost his baggage crossing the Wash and died in a seizure shortly afterwards. His nine-year-old son was crowned as Henry III and many barons, whose struggle had been based on their hatred of King John, now felt nothing but embarrassment from the presence of Louis. But he was still a force to be reckoned with and the fight continued. It was settled by the defeat of the baronial faction at Lincoln and the repulse of a further French invasion fleet off Dover.

The story of this latter event, which was the first occasion that an invader was actually destroyed at sea, has something of the bizarre about it. The French navy had already sustained a defeat by the Earl of Salisbury's fleet in 1213 and was apparently short of a competent admiral. At this moment along came Eustace the Monk, a French mercenary who had begun his life as a monk in Spain, but after dabbling in black magic and conspiracy had become a freebooting sailor. He served for a time under King John, then changed sides and joined the French. He assembled the fleet of several hundred vessels which put Prince Louis ashore in Kent and then took advan-

tage of his position to practise open piracy on traders who had
the misfortune to sail through the Channel. In 1217 when
Louis's position in England was rapidly becoming untenable,
he sent for reinforcements from France. Obligingly Eustace
produced a fleet, alleged to be a hundred strong, and set out for
England. Against this, England could muster a mere sixteen
vessels. Undoubtedly Eustace had more craft but most of
them were overloaded cumbersome transports; furthermore
the disparity in numbers is a little too large for even the most
enthusiastic patriot to swallow.

The battle took an unusual course in that the unloaded
English ships stood off at first, moving up wind. Then, when
in a favourable position, they swooped down on the lumber-
ing French craft. As they closed they launched sackloads of
quicklime into the wind blowing over the French ships.
Quicklime was a great favourite in medieval warfare. It
blinded opponents and proved distinctly uncomfortable when
it penetrated through the chinks of armour. But quicklime was
not the only weapon. The English ships (known as 'cogs')
were equipped with 'castles', which were large structures
afore and astern. They were a development from the fighting
deck of Alfred's navy and owed something to the use of the
lofty castle in land warfare. From these platforms, the forecastle and sterncastle, English archers sent volley after volley
of rope-cutting arrows into the French rigging. Ships were
then boarded, masts hacked down, crews slaughtered. It was a
bloody and unpleasant scene. Eustace tried to disguise himself
but was soon found and executed. As a native of Picardy he
was hardly a traitor but that fact did not save him. It was a
minor battle, but a great event in English naval history for it
marked the first resounding victory over an invader at sea.
Tactically it was a forerunner of other naval battles in which
superior manoeuvring and handling would enable the English
to fight at a distance, first with catapults, later with cannon, so
that finally they could close with and board the battered
enemy ships.

Naval warfare evolved slowly. Ships tended to be top-
heavy, too broad in the beam for speed, and smaller than a
hundred tons. They were too slow to be used for ramming, a
form of warfare which had been used very successfully with

swifter craft in the Mediterranean. But the general lawlessness of the seas, particularly the Channel where pirates and smugglers abounded, meant that there was always a reservoir of experienced fighting men for larger battles. As a basis for national fleet there was the confederation of the Cinque Ports. In the early eleventh century, before the Norman arrival, the five ports of Hastings, New Romney, Hythe, Dover and Sandwich had been granted certain privileges in the way of tax exemption in return for undertaking to supply ships to the monarch when needed. The original five (*cinque*) were soon increased to seven by the addition of Rye and Winchelsea. Later these became the 'head ports' and had thirty other Kent and Sussex towns attached to them for the original purpose. Their prestige and privilege increased until the fourteenth century, but after that their contribution was more than matched from other ports and they themselves suffered the handicap of gradually being silted up. Dover alone remains important and the Lord Warden of the Cinque Ports, whose official residence is Walmer Castle, is also Constable of Dover Castle. As we see in a later chapter the Cinque Ports all carry traces of the fortifications which were necessary in their days of glory.

The Channel, which had been intermittently dangerous since the foundation of the Cinque Ports, became especially so when Philip VI ascended the French throne in 1328. At the time there was a thriving wool trade between England and Flanders. Philip encouraged a considerable fleet of ships to prey on the ships engaged in it.

The English were at first ill-prepared for this warlike activity and in March 1338 suffered a humiliating defeat when a French fleet landed at Portsmouth and plundered and burnt the town. In October of the same year it was Southampton's turn for similar treatment. But in the following year the English were able to retaliate and inflict devastating casualties and damage on Le Tréport and Boulogne. This naval conflict, which continued with a series of minor but savage raids and battles, was linked with the larger struggle between Edward III of England and Philip which had already included an abortive invasion attempt by Edward. This had been launched from Flanders but after failing to capture Cambrai he returned to England for more money and stores. Meanwhile Philip had assembled a large fleet at Sluys with the intention of conquering Flanders and then invading England. By midsummer 1340 he had two hundred ships and an army of 20,000. The quality of his invasion force was not high, for those who could sail were not trained fighters and the soldiers had no experience at sea. At that time Sluys (which is now well inland) was an important port guarding the estuary of the Scheldt and Zwijn. The French were exulting over the five English merchantmen they had captured earlier and, fearing an attempt to rescue these, had deployed their fleet in three divisions (which was exactly how men were positioned for land battles).

Edward assembled a similar number of ships but proceeded warily. He found the French ships not only closely packed but also linked with chains to prevent the English breaking through. Against this naval fortress he had a superb weapon in the archers who were later to win battles at Crécy and Poitiers. These managed to inflict wholesale slaughter on the first line of French ships while the second and third lines could do little to retaliate. After causing heavy casualties Edward's force retired. The French emerged to follow, but once in the open received similar treatment in turn. To add to French discomfiture they were also attacked in the rear by the Flemings who hated them. Fugitives who struggled to land met an unpleasant but predictable fate.

It was a devastating though unexpected victory. Once again it underlined the supremacy of manoeuvre combined with some form of artillery, even though only arrows. The French made no effort to restore their naval challenge. Thus when Edward decided to invade France six years later he met no opposition when he landed his army in the Cotentin Peninsula and sacked Barfleur and Cherbourg.

Subsequently when Edward met the land armies of France at Crécy and Poitiers he found them equally immobile and a perfect target for his archers. Although the Battle of Sluys gave the English superiority in the Channel for a decade in the first part of the fourteenth century, naval rivalry was to continue for another five centuries. In 1350 there was a considerable naval battle off Winchelsea, which the English won, but nine years later a force of 3,000 Frenchmen landed at Winchelsea, slaughtered the citizens some of whom had hopefully taken refuge in the church, and then sacked and burnt the town. The raids continued. In 1377 Rye and Hastings were burnt; Portsmouth was burnt but its citizens beat back the invaders; Poole and the Isle of Wight were raided. Southampton drove off the attack in the roads outside the harbour. In 1385 and 1386 it seemed as if England might be invaded in spite of the fact that the English held Calais.

In 1416, the year after Henry V's devastating victory at Agincourt, the French blockaded Portsmouth and the Isle of Wight. In 1473 Southampton was the target, but swift action by the English fleet forced the French away.

Needless to say the raiding was by no means one-sided. The French often found themselves attacked by motley contingents of ships, some containing pirates, some Englishmen, and some Frenchmen from other areas. Law and order were difficult enough to enforce on land and virtually impossible at sea, even in territorial waters. A party of marauders which included Austrians set out from Dover and Sandwich in 1513 and plundered parts of Flanders. The French responded the following year with attacks on Brighton and Dover. But the same year saw the launching of Henry VIII's great 1,500-ton ship, the *Henry Grâce à Dieu* (the *Great Harry*), the most powerful vessel in the world at the time. Its size made it unsuitable for the Cinque Ports and thus further diminished their importance.

Soon Henry needed all the ships he could muster, for daring pirates were more active than ever during his reign. 1527 saw the Flemish ships capture a ship moored *inside* Southampton harbour. Ten years later Calshot Castle was built to prevent such humiliation occurring again. When Henry was excommunicated in 1538 and thus had the greatest powers in the world ranged against him, he ordered more castles and more ships.

In the previous chapter we mentioned the attack of 1545. It began on 18th July and the 225 ships, mostly French, included twenty-five oared galleys from the Mediterranean; thus when the British fleet lay becalmed at Spithead these were able to move freely and to pour shot after shot into Henry's navy. The *Great Harry* was almost sunk at anchor. A long-awaited breeze then sprang up and enabled the English frigate to manoeuvre. Unfortunately the same breeze capsized the *Mary Rose*, which apparently had all the portholes open. Seven hundred men were drowned.

The French retreated to the Isle of Wight, where they landed 2,000 troops. They met strong local resistance but did immense damage before they rejoined their ships.

Ships had clearly developed enormously in the two hundred years before 1540. The medieval cog was steered by a heavy oar let down from the side and had forecastle, aftercastle and even a small topcastle at the masthead. It was double-ended. It gave way to the nef which had a rudder at the stern supported on the sternpost. The 'castles' which had at first been temporary were now incorporated in the structure. But even greater changes came with the development of the naval gun.

Guns had been carried on ships from the fourteenth century but as their power increased it became necessary to provide a difference in design between the gun-carrying warship and the ordinary trader. Some of the early guns were muzzle-loaders, carried in cradles. The bore was about five inches. Too large a charge meant that the gun would explode killing all those around it. Early 'shot' was stone but later this was replaced by iron. These guns fired through portholes but between shots had to be retracted for reloading. There were also breech loaders but these were nearly as likely to blow out the back of the gun as to expel the shot from the barrel. However by the mid-fifteenth century a greater degree of all-round efficiency had been achieved. The influence of the long, fast Venetian galleys was soon seen in the newer ships of the English navy; the pattern was for longer, narrower, faster ships with lower superstructures. This was the type of ship which had caused an English naval disaster in 1545, but Henry's navy was quick to learn and although they did not go back to oared ships they incorporated the design of these faster craft. It might be claimed with some truth that the setbacks of 1545 enabled the English to beat the Armada, for without the earlier experience English ships could well have been nearly as cumbersome as their Spanish adversaries.

There was, inevitably, much conflict of opinion between the advocates of different designs of ship. The earlier type was known as the carrack; the later ones were galleons. Galleons were often smaller than their predecessors, being about 100 feet long and 30 feet wide. Their armament consisted of twenty muzzle-loading cannon which fired an 18-pound shot, and there would be twenty or thirty guns of smaller calibre firing 5- to 10-pound shot; the latter were mounted on the upper deck. There were too many different types of gun, and this created problems over the storage and carriage of ammunition. The ships' complement was about 150; for close-quarter fighting this was not enough but for every other activity it seemed to produce overmuch congestion. However, this was vastly preferable to the manning of Spanish ships which were overloaded with soldiers who could not sail and sailors who could not fight.

Progress continued, and in the seventeenth century ships were built with three masts (for a variety of sails), three decks, and 100 guns. This design with a few additions and modifications lasted till the mid-nineteenth century. The above dimensions were for capital ships but there was also a variety of smaller craft which became known as frigates, corvettes, or sloops. Nearly all tended to be overgunned. Ships are 'rated' according to size and armament. A typical warship of the late seventeenth century of the first rate would be about 135 feet long, 47 feet broad, with a draught of 19 feet and a weight of 1,600 tons; it carried 100 guns and had a complement of 600–800 men according to whether it was peace or war and where she was stationed. A sixth-rate ship would be a mere 140 tons and carried sixty men and fifteen guns. Generally speaking, there were eight men to each of the larger guns and three to one of the smaller ones. When England found herself engaged in the foolish and unnecessary Dutch Wars in the second half of the seventeenth century, the Dutch ships were better prepared (though slightly slower than the English) for the Dutch sailors had had considerable experience of fighting the Spanish. From now onwards we can see how the Royal Navy generally kept ahead of its rivals, partly by better design and partly by better seamanship. At intervals it absorbed some hard lessons and the hard knocks that went with them. The principal lesson was that flexibility and adaptability must never be impeded by tradition — however valuable that tradition in design. When the navy ignored this obvious lesson it was confronted with such events as the Battle of Jutland in World War I and the loss of the *Prince of Wales* and *Repulse* in World War II.

Many of the naval terms which were used in the age of sail and wooden ships have passed into the language as colloquialisms; unfortunately their use today is often derogatory. It was in fact no disgrace to be a sailor on a fifth-rate ship, even though you might occasionally be three sheets in the wind and thereafter be on your beam ends.

One of the more humiliating lessons learnt by the navy was taught by Van Tromp, the Dutch admiral, in the Battle of Dungeness, in 1652. The British were outnumbered and outgunned, but they were also outmanoeuvred. The Dutch captured two English ships and sank three more, all for the loss of one of their own. It was said that Van Tromp tied a broom to his masthead signifying he had swept the English from the seas but there is some doubt about this story. In any event the scores were levelled the following March when the English waylaid a large Dutch convoy, and scattered it. Even so, the Dutch were sufficiently dominant in the Channel to lie off Dover and bombard the harbour. In June the Battle of the North Foreland saw the Dutch defeated and Van Tromp killed. The victory was a narrow one, for the Dutch sent in fireships in the final stages and caused further English losses. The achievements of fireships in naval history deserves more credit than it has received, for they appeared, century after century, often frustrating invasion attempts, and their crews displayed amazing courage and skill.

Further reverses occurred in the Dutch War of 1665-7, notably when De Ruyter took a fleet up the Medway and burnt English ships in the Chatham dockyard. He also sent a fleet up the Thames and blockaded London. The fault was Charles II's, for he had neglected to repair the English ships after the victory off Lowestoft in 1665; however, by some adroit diplomacy he managed to secure a peace treaty which not only ended the war but also caused the Dutch to cede a colony in North America; it included the township of New Amsterdam which then became New York.

Gradually Anglo-Dutch rivalry was overlooked for the

needs of an even more dangerous struggle against the rise of an all-powerful France. It was ended officially when James II was deposed and William, Prince of Orange, who was married to a Stuart, accepted the English crown. In 1690 the French attempted to restore James II — an enterprise which led to the Battle of Beachy Head which the French ultimately lost. A feature of this battle was the daring of Jean Bart, a French naval adventurer in the best tradition, who explored the Beachy Head anchorage by posing as a fisherman; he counted the English ships and noted many other useful points about them. Were he alive today he would be interested in the activities of Eastern European fishing fleets, not to mention meteorological and marine survey ships. Jean Bart distinguished himself again in 1693 but even this did not raise French naval morale after they had lost fifteen major ships to an English fireship raid on the harbour of La Hogue (at Saint Vaast).

There were of course many other battles, such as that of Vigo Bay in 1702, but as these did not affect invasion plans they are not relevant here.

In 1758, in the early stages of the Seven Years War, the French mustered a force of 17,000 men at Morbihan, in Brittany. The aim was to effect simultaneous landings in the Thames and in Western Scotland. The situation was being carefully monitored by Admiral Hawke but on 14th October 1759 heavy gales forced Hawke to relinquish his grip and fall back to shelter at Torbay. The French slipped out of harbour but off Quiberon Bay encountered Hawke. The weather had eased, but had now become bad again, so bad in fact that the French admiral, Conflans, was confident that his fleet was safe from Hawke if he kept close inshore among the reefs and shallows. But he reckoned without Hawke's persistence and daring. Although the British admiral lost two ships, he displayed such boldness and skill that he completely destroyed the French fleet and with it French hopes of escorting an invasion flotilla.

In the eighteenth century some of the most popular ships were the third-raters which had two decks and carried 74 guns. They were 151 feet long and 43 feet in the beam. Armament consisted of 24-pounders and 12-pounders. Their successes against larger foreign ships were so numerous that 'the 74' became a household word. They were ably supported by another famous generation of third-raters — the 64s. Nelson commanded one of the latter in the Mediterranean, the *Agamemnon*. There were also 50s, 44s and even 22s. Readers of naval history — and fiction — will be familiar with the term 'man-of-war' which described any warship, including the smaller ones. Among these latter, brigs, sloops and cutters carried less than twenty guns; the cutters were particularly useful for coastal work — and were thus used by customs officers — but were seldom comfortable, and were unsuitable for rough water.

Steam was introduced to fighting ships in the mid-nineteenth century, when the screw propeller was perfected. This meant changes in design, and in general meant a smaller ship could be used for the same firepower. Some ships were built for both steam and sail. This was the heyday of the gunboat. They were squarely built and of shallow draught, carried four or five guns, and were ideal for work in rivers and estuaries.

By the end of the nineteenth century, when they gave way to the ironclads, the 'wooden walls of England' had completed a magnificent tour of service in frustrating would-be invaders. Perhaps their finest hour had been in the Napoleonic Wars. In 1797 six fleets were constantly blockading the ports of the Texel, Brest, Cadiz, Ferrol, Cartagena and Toulon. If one fleet had failed in its task, its French counterpart would have been able to sail to another port and thus create two-to-one supremacy. Once that had happened, invasion would have become a certainty. At the two battles of Camperdown and Cape St Vincent in 1797 the French nearly succeeded but ultimately were decisively defeated. The Battle of the Nile in 1798 failed to prevent the French invasion of Egypt but so isolated the French army there that Napoleon eventually deserted it and returned to France. Soon afterwards, in 1801, Nelson broke up a hostile coalition of Russia, Denmark and Sweden, in the Battle of Copenhagen.

The moment of greatest peril came in 1803 when Napoleon decided to settle Britain once and for all with invasion. But two years later, before even Trafalgar was fought, he had decided that there was no chance of achieving the local naval superiority he needed.

Through the remainder of the nineteenth century the fact that the British navy was the most powerful navy in the world did more than all the shore forts and installations to save Britain from invasion. Nor was the importance of the navy lessened with the development of more powerful guns and more sophisticated craft. The ironclad Dreadnoughts of the early years of the present century were a formidable threat — but only against nations with similar thinking. The new enemy was Germany; the old enemy, France, was now an ally. The Dreadnoughts had ten 12-inch guns, although only four could be trained in the same direction. However they still supplied a massive broadside. They were followed by a class of battle cruiser which had eight guns only but all could fire in the same direction when a broadside was required. The Dreadnought had a speed of 21 knots, the battle-cruisers 26. During World War I naval warfare was curiously static for large ships. The only great battle was at Jutland in 1916, when British losses were heavier than German. However, the German High Seas Fleet retired to port and the strategic victory was with the British. Considerably more activity was seen with smaller craft, notably submarines (U-boats) and their hunters. The Channel was guarded by the Dover Patrol, which consisted of a miscellany of ships and protected the endless traffic between Britain and France.

By World War II the Royal Navy had adapted itself to a war which would be different from any other — its part in that war will be described in a later chapter. Subsequently the shape, role, and size of the navy has been dramatically changed. However its importance as an anti-invasion force is likely to continue to be as important as ever, even in the days of heavy air transport.

Throughout its history the Royal Navy has had a role which transcends its function. It has been a symbol of all that is good in Britain. Its efficiency, the manner in which it wielded the most unpromising material (often recruited through press gangs) into superb fighting crews, the daring of its captains and its supreme imperturbability have given it a reputation which has made it a mould for those of many other nations. Yet in the last few years governments have tended to be at first vacillating, then parsimonious, in provision for the Royal Navy. Unfortunately, the Russians realize only too well the importance of a powerful fleet and encourage theirs accordingly. In the 1980s we should do well to bear in mind the words of Sir George Savile in the seventeenth century:

'The Importance of being strong at sea was ever very great, so in our present Circumstances it is grown very much greater; because as formerly our force in shipping contributed greatly to our Trade and Safety, so now it is become indispensably necessary to our very being.

It may be said now to England thou art busy about many things but one thing is necessary. To the question, What shall we do to be saved in this World there is no other answer but this, Look to your Moat.'

4 The Traces of Invasion

Everywhere in Britain there are signs of attempted invasions and they take many forms. One of the most interesting effects of past history is the physical appearance of the inhabitants of these islands. Even today, after there has been much inter-breeding, certain tribal characteristics stand out as clearly as ever in certain areas. Obvious examples of Iberian descent may be found in Cornwall and South Wales, of Celts in North Wales and Scotland, of Scandinavians in Yorkshire and Saxons in Hampshire. However, in this book we are concerned with physical marks on the landscape rather than on the human body.

Some of those traces go back so far that we cannot even guess by whom and against whom they were made. They include St David's Head in Dyfed (Pembrokeshire) which consists of three lines of defence, walls and ditches, with a single narrow entrance. It is a simple but frequently used form of fortification, for it utilizes three sides of a natural defence (a spur of land) and makes an artificial barrier on the fourth. Later, the Normans used the same device frequently to make sites for castles, as at Hastings and Kenilworth. Cornwall has a similar but stronger defence at Trevelgay (Originally Trevel-gue) Head, two miles to the east of Newquay. Trevelgay has seven lines of ramparts and ditches. Treryn Dinas, five miles from Land's End, has three lines of ramparts. Tintagel, which for long was thought to be a Norman creation, dates back to a much earlier period, and, like the others mentioned here, is pre-Iron Age, and possibly 2000 BC.

A problem with ancient sites is that they may have been

used for later military requirements and been altered beyond ready recognition. Archaeologists can usually date the component parts and do magnificent work in identification. However, some archaeologists adopt defensive omniscience about sites with which they are concerned, and reject any historical or military observation. The fact that these were defences established for a military purpose during a period of historical disturbance does not appear to them to be as important as what remains on the site today. This seems to have led to a private vocabulary, which uses the term 'ring-work' for outer defences. It may be a convenient generalization but it is sheer nonsense in a military historical description.

As we saw earlier, we owe a debt to archaeologists for discovering that Crickley Hill was once the scene of a Neolithic battle. It may well be that similar sites will be discovered elsewhere, particularly as the skills of aerial photography are developing so rapidly. It is probable that every hill-top once held a minor fortification, however simple. Some of the ancient hill forts in Britain are known as causewayed camps and it is assumed that their sole use was for corralling cattle against wild animals at night. It is interesting to think that at one period at least in the history of man he was able to live without apprehension of violence from his neighbours, but one needs to be somewhat of an idealist to believe it. Today's child will leap on any mound and declaim to its playmates, 'I'm the king of the castle and you are the dirty rascal'. Were our ancestors so different?

The Iron Age, which was long thought to have begun in about 700 BC is now thought to date from at least two hundred years earlier. As far as is known there were three distinct waves of settlers in the period; presumably their rivalry led to the building of the surprisingly large numbers of forts we can identify. In all there are believed to be at least two thousand Iron Age forts in Britain and their location may easily be found from the Ordnance Survey Map *Southern Britain in the Iron Age*. It extends from the Isle of Wight to Scarborough and includes Wales and Cornwall, so the definition of 'Southern Britain' may not suit everyone; nevertheless it is a most valuable and interesting map and a tribute to the skill and foresight of those who produced it.

As may be expected there is no standard pattern of hill fort in the way that there was often a standard pattern of fortifications like Martello towers. Hill forts varied according to the contours of the ground, the direction of expected attack, the number of people available to construct them and, probably, special ideas of long dead tacticians. One aspect of their appearance today is deceptive in that the outer defences appear to consist of sloping banks. Some of the banks probably did slope but many were vertical and were held that way by revetting — i.e. enclosed by timber. It was possible to make a fort reasonably quickly by building a palisade of tree trunks just below the summit of a hill, then creating a step above it by filling in the inner side with material dug from further up. Then a second layer could be added below the first palisade. Of course, if the palisades were not renewed, weathering would in time — perhaps a century or so of rain — wash the hill-top smooth again and only faint outer traces would remain of what had once been a formidable fortress; underneath the surface, however, will be some remains of the tree trunks.

Iron Age forts were particularly strong in the gateways. Here the unwelcome intruder would receive his hottest reception and perhaps also be lured to destruction down a blind alley. All through the time in which swords, spears and shields were used there was always a turning to the right designed to put the attacker at a disadvantage. With the shield on his left arm, the oncoming warrior would open a gap between his sword arm and his shield as he made the half-turn right. At the same time his sword arm would be impeded by its proximity to the right-hand wall. Excellent use of this factor was made in medieval castles where most of the staircases spiral upwards to the right. The ascender has all the handicaps, including that of catching his arm on the central pillar, while the defender has both height and free mobility for his right arm.

The presence of high walls in Iron Age forts made some form of howitzer essential. Howitzers were widely used in World War I when it was essential to have a gun with a high trajectory which could lob shells over obstacles into enemy trenches. Trench mortars are a similar weapon — and very disconcerting it can be to find that what appeared to be a protective bank presents no obstacle at all to a trench mortar bomb. In the Iron Age lack of concentrated power was compensated for by quantity. The sling was known to be one of the most deadly weapons long before the Iron Age, and its use was continued well into medieval times. Apparently the Balearic Islanders were particularly adept with this weapon; it is recorded that children were not allowed to have food before they could hit it with a stone slung from a suitable distance. This can have offered little encouragement to breast feeding. Doubtless David's feat against Goliath was not considered unduly surprising in Biblical times. To judge from the number of slingstones scattered around Iron Age forts, and also the large caches of them which have been found, the slinger must have been one of the most important of the earlier warriors. His ammunition was cheap, expendable, portable and deadly. A skilled slinger could probably project several stones at once, and as accuracy was not as important as frequency in this form of attack a few hundred slingers could make life intolerable behind the ramparts. Slingers must also have influenced the type and height of barricade on top of the ramparts; at a certain height the trajectory necessary to clear the obstacle would also take it well behind the defenders. The size and number of any post holes on top of the rampart would give a clue to the effectiveness of this type of attack.

The slingstones — and sling bullets of baked clay — were eventually supplanted by the arrow, probably because the arrow had the greater penetrative power. But the value of a stone (often miscalled a 'rock') as a missile has continued up to modern times. It is particularly effective in times of civil disorder when mobs of insurgents hurl bottles, tins and above all stones at the forces of law and order.

The construction of the hill forts — and later the motte and bailey castles — has been the subject of considerable unintelligent speculation. Archaeology has now gone metric — heaven help us — and one reads about ramparts 4–6 metres high enclosing areas of 4.8 hectares. These will doubtless be useful descriptive terms when we start exporting Iron Age forts and have to fill in customs declarations but until that time arrives it might be better to stick to feet and inches. Most British measurements, such as the foot, date back at least to Roman times because they are essentially recognizable and practical, trendy

Maiden Castle, Dorset

Types of flint arrowhead: from left to right, barbed; tanged
and barbed; single-tanged

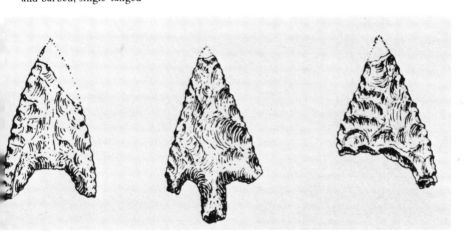

Hadrian's Wall from the west of Housestead Fort

The Roman fort at Richborough in Kent

Part of the Bayeux Tapestry depicting William arriving at Bayeux

English labourers building a fort at Hastings, from the Bayeux Tapestry

Bodiam Castle, Sussex, an early anti-invasion measure

Deal Castle, a Henry VIII fort with a very modern look

Dover Castle

The landgate at Rye

A cog, a double-ended sailing ship with a steering oar, developed in the 12th and 13th centuries

Opposite a medieval siege machine in action

The army on its way, from the Bayeux Tapestry

'Fireworks from Gonnes and Bowes', from Smith's *Art of Gunnery*, 1643

archaeologists should note.

A general assumption is that Iron Age forts took decades to build. It seems unlikely. Naive deductions were made from an experiment conducted a few years ago at Overton Down. Deer antler picks were used with other primitive tools and it was calculated that a man could move up to 1½ cubic yards of chalk per day. Neolithic man, who was accustomed to the task and the tools, could probably accomplish that in an hour, depending on the urgency of the situation. Doubtless the volunteers who worked in the Overton experiment imagined they were doing their best. However, it might have been a different story if an overseer had pricked them with half an inch of spear point every time they straightened their backs. Likewise it seems improbable that the Normans who erected mottes at speed wherever they went would have seen eye to eye with modern trade union ideas of the norm for a day's work on a building site. Iron Age tools, although lacking the finish of modern implements, were no doubt adequate for the purpose. Much might be learnt from the survivors of the trench diggers of World War I. On the great retreat of 1914 men dug into the chalk with mess tins and jack-knives; their trenching tools had been left behind in the cause of greater mobility. Few things can be less suitable than an army mess tin for digging holes in chalk — but, then, it was done under shellfire.

Undoubtedly hill forts received additions and repairs century after century. In World War II anti-aircraft detachments and units making preparations for home defence were often surprised to find that the site *they* had selected as being of strategic or tactical importance had had previous occupants. Thus a fort which had been begun in 600 BC might have been used by Britons against Romans, by Saxons against Danes, by English against Normans, and prepared over and over again for hostilities against French, Spanish and Germans.

Although some of the earliest Iron Age settlements appear to have been in Yorkshire, such as Scarborough, the ones of the main invasion routes are inevitably in the south. When Caesar landed in 54 BC he found it necessary to capture Big-berry in Kent, three miles west of Canterbury. This had been built about four hundred years earlier, doubtless against another invasion threat. Unfortunately, Bigberry has been much damaged in recent times by gravel pits and roads but enough remains to show that this was once a formidable obstacle enclosing some thirty acres. Among the relics produced by excavation are slave neck-irons, which suggests that the construction of the fort was not done by volunteers.

There are a number of other substantial Iron Age forts along the line of the North Downs and close to the North Down Trackway (also called 'The Pilgrims Way') which continues into Wiltshire (where it is known as the Harroway). There is a huge fort at Oldbury (near Wrotham, Kent), another at Hulberry (near Abinger, Surrey), another at Keston (called, as many now are, Caesar's Camp), another at Squerryes Park (Westerham, Kent), and another at Cardinal's Cap (Caterham, Surrey). There is a large fort at Carshalton and smaller ones at Ewell and Weybridge. All these represent a form of defence in depth, for the invader having landed at Folkestone and come on to the trackway is now well on his way inland. When the country was still uncleared and undrained this was obviously a principal invasion route. In between the North and South Downs there was a network of streams, some of which ran into Rye Bay, and progress in such an area would be difficult.

The main fortifications on the South Down began at Beachy Head and ran through Seaford to Mount Caburn (near Lewes), Hollingbury, the Devil's Dyke, Cissbury Ring (near Worthing), Chanctonbury (near Washington), Halnaker Hill and The Trundle (near Goodwood) on to Old Winchester Hill and St Catherine's Hill, near Winchester. Again, there are many lesser forts which merit a visit.

As we move further west the number of large forts increases rapidly. Woodbury, Winklebury, Bullsdown (near Silchester), Beacon Hill, Sidbury, Ebsbury, Bratton Castle, Cadbury, Hod Hill, Badbury Rings, and numerous lesser fortifications, all show that, once established, the earlier invaders intended to hold their ground. By this time they were approaching the sea again and had no desire to be driven into it by successive waves of invaders. From here, all the way to Cornwall, one gets the impression of settlers standing to fight. There is a cluster of forts around Lyme Bay, beginning with the vast ramparts of Maiden Castle to the east (near Dorchester) and continuing

through Eggardon, Musbury, and Blackbury. To the north
are Ham Hill and Neroche. To the west many are smaller, such
as Castle Dore, but Carn Brea in Cornwall is as large as any
elsewhere. Some of these ancient forts are more accessible than
others but to examine the majority you need a strong pair of
legs and considerable determination.

Although most of the castles were built two or three
hundred years before the Romans arrived, their real test did
not come before Caesar landed. We have noted what happened
to Bigberry; Wheathampstead, where Cassivellaunus had set
up his headquarters, suffered a similar fate.

The later invasion under Aulus Plautius had to adopt a much
more concentrated approach to the subjection of the inhabitants of Britain. For that objective Plautius's successors
methodically captured forts as they came to them; it was not
always the largest which put up the most resistance. Often,
one British tribe held a number of forts and defended each
stubbornly in turn. It is thought that some tribes offered no
resistance because they were more happily disposed towards
the Romans with whom they already had trading links than to
their neighbours in adjacent territories. Others had an entirely
different attitude, for they included large numbers of refugees
from Caesar's territory of Gaul who had no wish to endure a
second period of Roman rule. By the time the Romans reached
Wales and attacked first the Silures in the south and then the
Deceangli and Ordovices in the north there were no easy
options left; every mile of territory they won was paid for with
blood. As long as there was unconquered territory the
Romans were still invaders. Only when they reached Scotland
and were finally checked did they cease to be attackers and
then instead became defenders, first behind the Antonine Wall
and then behind Hadrian's Wall.

Owing to somewhat misleading 'artists' impressions' in
children's history books there is a widespread belief that the
Romano-British battles occupied at most a few hundred men.
Such a view is far removed from the truth. It is now believed
that against the Romans' 40,000 the Britons could and did put
into the field 60–80,000. This suggests that when they fell back
to the hill forts these were fully manned, large though they
were. There is, unfortunately, no full account of a Roman

assault on a British hill fort, though there are several accounts of Roman siege technique as practised in other countries. Undoubtedly there were desperate battles around the hill forts in Wessex which were captured by Vespasian. The key to Roman success was no doubt a combination of better training and better equipment. Had they wished, the Romans could doubtless have besieged and starved out the inhabitants of the hill forts, who seldom seem to have had access to adequate water supplies. But the Romans preferred a swift and bloody fight. The gateway of any fortification is paradoxically the strongest and the weakest point. It is the weakest in that it is a break in the general line of fortification but it may also be the strongest in that it is ably and cunningly defended with traps, warriors, and multivallate lines. After a few feint attacks on the outer lines the Romans would hurl their main effort at the gate. For this they had heavy siege machinery which could throw a heavy stone and smash a wooden barrier, ballistas which could direct a giant terrifying javelin into the heart of the defence, and the testudo, a cover of shields which would enable the legionaries to approach the gate unharmed (almost) by missiles hurled on to them from above. Above all it was sheer professional training which enabled the Roman soldier to win his battles. Training was endless and the legionary could handle his weapons as deftly as a first-class tennis player uses a racket. Every soldier carried two long stakes which had a multiplicity of uses; their most frequent employment was for supporting a temporary defence which would enable the soldier to crawl up closely to his objective or resist a counter-attack if one came. At Spettisbury Rings, in Dorset, a few miles south-east of Blandford, there are ninety skeletons most of which had Roman weapons embedded in the bones. This must literally have been a fight to the finish. We have often heard of the order to fight to the last man and the last bullet, but it is seldom carried out fully. But with or without orders the hill fort of Spettisbury was defended to the last sword thrust. Some of the forts, such as Hembury, in Devon, bear traces of fire, suggesting that the Romans used the time-honoured method of throwing combustible material against the gate.

But the Romans in their turn became defenders, not attackers. They maintained a Channel fleet to intercept Saxon raiders, they built first Hadrian's Wall and then the Antonine against invaders from the north, and they had a complex system of military outposts along the Welsh Marches. A march is a border state; here it was the line from Chester to Newport. In Germany the 'Mark', i.e. border state, of Brandenburg became the foundation of Prussia and its attendant militarism. Usually the people who live in marches or marks prefer activity to a quiet life, and when they are there have little further choice in the matter.

The Romans believed in the value of walls as anti-invasion measures but did not, of course, consider them to be complete protection. Their idea was to have concentrations of troops at mileposts and to bring a concentration of fire power on to a threatened point. It is a sound military principle to concentrate your force, and if you can bring pressure to bear suddenly you may also achieve surprise as well.

The custom of building vast walls seems strange today but it was widely practised in the early period of history. Not only did the Romans build walls in Britain, they also built the Limes Germanicus from Coblenz to the Danube, with the aim of holding back the barbarians (as they referred to their unconquered foes). There were other equally formidable walls built by the Romans in the Middle East but their effect on invaders was minimal.

Walls have been built throughout history, right up to the present day, though the Berlin Wall, the latest, is not a military obstacle, but is merely effective against civilian refugees. The last great defensive wall was the West Wall, built by the Germans with conscripted labour along the coastline of Normandy; there are many traces left. A few years earlier great faith had rested in the Maginot Line, which the French had hoped would keep out the Germans, but a wall is only as good as the people who garrison it and the French in the line had no heart for the task.

Inevitably there is some mystery attached to ancient earth walls whose builders are long since dead. For many years people have been puzzled by the purpose of the Devil's Dyke in Suffolk, of which there are seven miles between Reach and Ditton Green on the Cambridgeshire border, but it is now realized that it belongs to the era when the inhabitants of East Anglia saw danger not from the east but the west. Recent aerial photography has revealed the existence of another long and formidable barrier which once virtually separated the East Anglian area from the rest of the country. It appears to be neolithic. Another mysterious earthwork lies further west. This is Grim's Dyke, in the Chilterns. It is thought to have been built by the Saxons. Some of the earthworks in East Anglia and elsewhere are believed to have been built by and against the Belgae, a warlike tribe, a mixture of Teuton and Celt, who invaded this country shortly before the Romans came. Their capital was Colchester, called after Camulos, their god of war.

Although there is considerable uncertainty about the age and purpose of the ancient earth boundaries there is much less about the so-called 'Forts of the Saxon Shore'. These have already been mentioned in connection with the ambition, life, and death of their designer, the Roman provincial emperor Carausius. There were probably eleven originally but two have apparently disappeared into the encroaching sea. Those left are in various degrees of preservation. The nine are: Brancaster, Burgh, Bradwell, Reculver, Richborough, Dover, Lympne, Pevensey and Portchester. Each guarded a potential invasion route and each made a base for the Roman anti-raider fleet. An interesting feature is that all had heavy mountings for ballistas. These are particularly noticeable at Portchester. Ballistas were heavy catapults which could hurl large stones considerable distances. Any large ships contemplating entering harbour and disembarking hostile troops would probably have been sunk by huge stones smashing through their hulls. At close range shore-based artillery, which can afford to be heavier than its waterborne equivalent, is more than a match for potential opponents.

Of Brancaster, near Hunstanton in Norfolk, nothing worth seeing remains, but Burgh, Suffolk, is a different matter altogether. Here some of the remaining walls are still fifteen feet high. They are eleven feet wide at the base and taper to six feet at the top. The area of the enclosure is about five acres. Burgh is a curiously beautiful ruin.

Bradwell, on the estuary of the Blackwater, is dwarfed by

the nearby nuclear power station. However, there is more to see here than there is at Reculver which has been badly eroded by the sea. Reculver guarded what was once the navigable waterway Wantsum; this separated the shoreline from the Isle of Thanet. The ruins of a Saxon church now stand on the site.

Next comes Richborough, which was once a very important Roman supply base. Although it became one of Carausius' forts of the Saxon shore, much of the work here is earlier. There is an excellent museum by the gateway.

The Roman fort at Dover, alas, is no more; it has disappeared under the town buildings. But the Romans have an enduring monument in the lighthouse, the Pharos, which now stands in the medieval castle. There is also archaeological evidence of a massive Roman catapult which could throw a heavy stone distances up to a mile.

Little remains of Lympne but Pevensey, in Sussex, compensates for losses elsewhere. Pevensey, for which the Roman name was Anderida, has had a long and turbulent history. When it was built in the third century AD the sea came up to its walls. It is large, enclosing ten acres, with walls fifteen feet high and twelve feet thick. It is possible to see why it was such a formidable fortification in the hands of the Romans. It watched over a beach which has always been regarded as one of the main invasion routes. When it was built ships could sail close up to the walls into its harbour but unfortunately the sea has now receded and it is not possible to visualize how tactically sound the setting was. Some of the Britons who were left defenceless after the Roman withdrawal in the fifth century made a terrible mistake when they took refuge in Pevensey and were besieged by the Saxons. All were massacred. Fixed defences are a deathtrap unless they are adequately garrisoned and provisioned and there is some safe means of exit should the position become untenable.

The Normans quickly recognized the usefulness of Pevensey. It seems probable that William I used it when he landed in 1066; certainly the Normans were quick to build a strong castle there. The Norman castle saw fighting in medieval times, and was prepared for more in 1940 when carefully camouflaged machine-gun posts were built into the structure. Needless to say, the guns have long since disappeared but their mounting is clearly visible and is an interesting example of military continuity which extends to some 1,700 years.

Portchester, already briefly mentioned, is probably the best preserved of the forts. It was perfectly sited for its original pupose but when weapons changed in later centuries became vulnerable. Fourteen of the original twenty bastion towers have survived, and show how effectively they could have been used, not only for ballista mountings but also to facilitate flanking fire along the walls. A tower which juts out enables a bowman (or rifleman) to fire laterally along the wall with a distinctly discouraging effect for an enemy engaged there. In medieval castles flanking fire was much assisted by arrow loops but even when directed from the top of the battlements was disconcerting and deadly.

Like many ancient castles Portchester became a prison after its military value had diminished. During the Dutch War of 1665–7 it housed Dutchmen, and in the Seven Years War (1756–63) Frenchmen. Frenchmen again were its unwilling occupants in the period of the Napoleonic Wars (1793–1815). Apparently they were overcrowded and underfed. They scratched their names on the walls as may be seen to this day. It is recorded that when a visitor who had come to see the governor tied up his horse at the gate he was astonished to find a few hours later that it had completely disappeared; it had already been eaten by the prisoners. Unlike Pevensey, Portchester was not called into service in World War II.

Cardiff Castle is built within the bounds of what was once a Roman shore fort, and a section of the old Roman wall is on view to visitors. There are Roman shore forts at Boulogne, Rouen, Bayeux, Coutances, Avranches, St Servan, Brest, Vannes, Nantes and Blaye. Having had the experience of invading so many countries themselves, the Romans were fully alert to the dangers of being invaded in their turn. The presence of a fort at Rouen indicates their appreciation of craft coming up the Seine — a blow to the heart if ever there was one.

Apart from their coastal forts the Romans had a valuable anti-invasion structure in their inland forts and excellent road system. If danger threatened troops could be moved rapidly from one area to another.

Unfortunately for the Britons the long period of Roman occupation allowed the native inhabitants to become soft and unmartial. Thus when the Saxons arrived in the third, fourth and fifth centuries, the Britons put up very little resistance in the south-east. In the west and in Wales the Saxons had to fight harder for their gains, as the battles of Baydon and Deorham testify. Ultimately the Saxons, Jutes and Angles became the dominant powers and invasion then meant incursions from Northumbria to Mercia, Wessex to Sussex, or counter-moves. East Anglia, Essex, Kent and Sussex were small in comparison with their vast neighbours such as Wessex, which extended from Devon to Kent; Mercia, which spanned the country from Chester to the Thames Valley; or Northumbria, which reached from the Humber to Scotland.

The next wave of invaders, the Vikings, caused the English to devise the burhs, forerunners of our modern boroughs, of which nothing remains except archaeological traces. Burhs were originally community refuges where temporary shelter could be taken behind a bank and a thorn thicket. Garrisoned by desperate people who know that surrender to the Vikings meant painful death with no alternatives, the burhs put up more resistance than the Vikings had time to overcome. In areas such as Somerset crannogs were an even more secure version of burhs.

In time the Vikings were absorbed and the next line of defences stem from the Norman Conquest. The Normans — the 'Northmen' — were the descendants of Vikings who had settled in France and while there had developed a form of fortification that had originated in Central Europe. It was the motte, a simple steep mound with a palisade on top. Giving it extra height was a wooden look-out tower which also formed a residence. Around the base was a ditch filled with sharp stakes, or water; later it was called the moat. Mottes were an ideal means of holding captured ground. They could be raised within a few days with impressed labour; one being built is depicted on the Bayeux Tapestry. They were sited where it was militarily most convenient to place them; the one at Oxford was built on demolished Saxon houses. Often they were planted in the middle of former fortresses, perhaps Roman camps, perhaps Iron Age forts, perhaps on a prehistoric burial mound. Most of them were well-constructed, but if over-hasty workmanship caused them to fall down they could soon be rebuilt. Sometimes they were built on natural hillocks, as at Windsor; sometimes in marshes, and sometimes on flat rocky ground where the wooden tower was soon replaced with a stone erection — the Tower of London was probably stone from the outset. Having been an invader himself, William the Conqueror had no wish to see the other side of the coin. As soon as he landed he began establishing mottes — the first is said to have been at Hastings though it may have been preceded by one at Pevensey. Very rapidly the country was covered with a network of mottes, blocking every bridge, ford, crossroads, valley entrance, hill pass, and estuary. The anti-invasion network took first priority and soon there was a chain of castles across the south coast, each a day's march from the other. Dover, Hastings, Eastbourne, Pevensey, Lewes, Bramber, Arundel, Portchester, Southampton, Christchurch, Wareham formed a first line; for the potential invader who broke through these there was another line from Canterbury, Tonbridge, Abinger, Farnham, Guildford, Winchester, Old Sarum, and dozens more which were smaller but would none the less be formidable obstacles. Along the east coast there would soon be a chain from Caister, Bungay, Framlingham, Orford, Colchester, Hadleigh. The establishment of a network of castles from Dover to Northumberland achieved a dual purpose of holding down the local people and, at the same time, making the task of another invader extremely difficult. A castle astride a trackway through a marsh *must* be reduced but its very position makes it difficult to assault. You cannot mine underneath it and blow it up for water will flood your diggings, you cannot comfortably sit and besiege it for you have not the time to sit around in that damp and disease-ridden spot, you cannot bring your full force to bear on it because the narrowness of the approach road prohibits it. If you are able to skirt around it you must leave a detachment of your men to keep an eye on it or you will find a raiding party will cut your line of communication with disastrous consequences. But if there are many of these castles in strategic spots — and that is where they will be — you will find that leaving these detachments so weakened your force that you will be outnumbered when you reach your final objective.

There they are still, after a thousand years of weathering. Some, like Arundel, have large palatial additions at the side; others like Lewes and Bramber are ruins but even after this length of time they leave the visitor in no doubt about their former strength. Should you wish to try climbing a motte there is ample opportunity at Bramber and nowadays no one will be directing arrows at you or showering you with red-hot sand. Even with the aid of a few brambles it is difficult to pull yourself up. A piece of the old masonry at Bramber over-hangs; it looks dangerous but it is unlikely to fall for it has been like that for several hundred years already. There is an even more dramatic overhang at Bridgnorth in Shropshire.

The castles inside the walls of Portchester and Pevensey were built after the Conqueror's day. Castles can be dated fairly easily. The very first are probably mere mounds but some have been converted to stone castles by building a wall around the summit. These are known as shell keeps. Some stone castles appear to be built on earth mounds but in fact the foundations extend through the mound to virgin soil. The first stone castles are rectangular with massive keeps like the Tower of London or Colchester. The walls are enormously thick and the corners square. Later corner towers and bastion towers were added, strengthening the structure and adding facilities for flanking fire. Later the gatehouse became immensely strong, as at Dover. Some of the castles fell into ruin once their military need was past but others were modi-fied to make them more comfortable though less defensible.

Note how cunningly they were sited. Lewes Castle was at the highest navigable point on the River Ouse and therefore controlled trade and shipping. It also monitored the gap through the Downs. Dover guarded what has aptly been described as the gateway of England, Arundel policed the Arun and Bramber the Adur.

Later in the Middle Ages when the French appeared to be threatening invasion, two more important castles were built. They were Queensborough (1361) and Bodiam (1385). Queensborough was built on the Isle of Sheppey but unfortu-nately did not survive the Civil War. Bodiam was built to guard the River Rother against invaders when Anglo-French tension was very great. Both castles were of open plan design. Throughout the Middle Ages castles had gradually become more complicated and the process culminated in the concentric design of castle like Harlech, and Beaumaris in North Wales. (The Tower of London is also concentric, as it is designed for the inner fortress to fire out over the outer lines.) Concentric castles were eventually found to be too complicated, for in order to frustrate attackers the interiors had been made so complicated that the defenders were themselves hampered in their movements. The outcome was a castle of simple design such as Bodiam with strong gatehouses and corner towers but also an uncluttered interior which would allow defenders to move rapidly from place to place as required. Today Bodiam (twelve miles north of Hastings) looks so peaceful and beautiful that it is difficult to imagine it was designed for a sterner purpose than elegant living. However, if a French raider had pushed up the river after a raid on Rye (nine miles south-east of it) he would have found it anything but serene.

It should never be forgotten that castles were essentially bases for mobile defence, not passive buildings waiting to be attacked. The effective patrolling area of a castle was twenty-five miles' radius and an invader could be engaged while he was still well out of sight of the defending castle.

Herstmonceux, built in 1441, was another castle built with an eye to a possible French invasion. Like Bodiam it is serenely beautiful but may surprise some visitors by the fact that it is built of brick. Brick was just coming in as a material for castles at this time. Herstmonceux is visitable but, as it also houses the Greenwich observatory, has strict limits on its times.

5 Walled Towns

Ships, castles and guns were one way of deterring invaders, another method was to fortify towns so that progress to strategic points would be slow. Some of the fortified towns in Britain grew up from the primitive Saxon burh, with not much more than a palisade and a ditch to protect them, but others, such as London, Colchester, Chester, Winchester and Exeter, already had walls dating from Roman times.

The Romans had ample experience of fortifying towns. Aosta, in northern Italy, still preserves many of the towers which once made this an important frontier town. Rome, as may be imagined, was even more formidable. It had a huge rectangular fort 481 yards by 415, surrounded by a battle-mented wall, and outer city walls 24 feet high. London was on a lesser scale but still enclosed 330 acres with walls eight feet thick. Unfortunately the height of the original walls is not known as only short portions remain above ground level; however forty feet may have been their height from ground level.

The Romans were by no means the pioneers of walled towns. There were many in the ancient world, and some are still to be seen. Babylon and Ur both had powerful fortifications in 2000 BC. Troy's first defences were even older, dating from 3000 BC. Mycenae and Tarragona are younger, both dating from 1500 BC. The walls of the latter were twenty feet thick and over thirty feet high.

As we saw earlier, the Anglo-Saxon kingdoms established great earthwork barriers to mark their boundaries and form a defensible frontier. Conflicts between the rival kings were decided by open battles rather than sieges of townships. The Anglo-Saxons had become an agricultural people, capable of establishing monasteries and market towns but for the most part being concerned with the husbandry of animals and fields. There was much pioneering to be done. When an area was cleared it was sometimes given the name of 'tun' or 'ton', thus when Wulfhere cleared a portion of thicket to make a farm this would become Wulfhere's tun and, later, Wolverton. Sometimes a place would be named after a family, 'an ing', and then would become a village, hamlet or township. Thus names like Birmingham (Beorma's people) came into being. Clearly these small settlements would be too thinly populated and isolated to defend themselves adequately. This did not matter until the arrival of the Vikings during the ninth century.

Viking methods of warfare have already been described; counter-measures took time and those same counter-measures were adopted by the Vikings to hold land they had overrun. The scarcity of land in Scandinavia and the potential richness of land in Britain made settlement seem entirely desirable. The Isle of Thanet and the Isle of Sheppey were obvious places for the Vikings to fortify themselves in while planning further conquests, but they built camps of palisades in other areas too, such as Derby, Stamford, Leicester, Lincoln and Nottingham. In the year 878 Alfred, who had been forced to retreat to the crannogs and marshes of Somerset, suddenly hit back. After his victory at Ashdown he wisely made peace and the first waves of the Vikings were accepted as joint holders of part of Britain.

A century later the situation was worse than ever. Alfred's strong rule had been followed by a succession of weaker kings. Fresh waves of Viking invaders suddenly realized that England was now a tempting and easy prey once more. There was no one of the stature of Alfred to rally the English this time. However, the English now saw that they must fend for themselves or perish. The occupants of towns applied themselves to make more effective defences than the old burh palisade. Huge earthworks were raised and on them were built daunting stockades. Sometimes the combination of wood and stone was burnt, intentionally or in battle, and the result was a solid mass of obstacle known as a 'vitrified' fort. But the advantages of a thorn palisade on a high bank should not be underrated. It could be more difficult to penetrate than a wall, and breaches could be repaired easily and cheaply. Thus to the later wave of invaders we owe some impressive tenth-century fortifications. Wallingford in Berkshire, Wareham in Dorset, and Maldon in Essex still have huge earthworks which were undoubtedly necessary. They were built by landholders who probably lived inside the burh and farmed land outside. Many of the earthworks had been begun in the earlier wave of the Viking invasions; they were now hastily improved and completed. There is a very interesting Anglo-Saxon document which bears the daunting title of the 'Burghal Hidage'. It covers the period 911–19 and it lists not only the fortified towns but also the numbers needed to man the walls. The name 'burh bot' was given to the system of furnishing labour and materials to build the fortifications. Once they were built it is probable that each family in the district would be allotted a section of the wall. The same principle was adopted later in 'castle-guard' in which one family might be responsible for one section of the battlements of a castle for generation after generation. Even today this system of supplementing payments with service is not entirely obsolete among ratepayers. Every town has its body of volunteers which will help clean a canal, organize Jubilee celebrations, or repair ancient monuments. The word 'hidage' is linked to the system of clearing land when this was a community effort. A hide was an area of land, of an average size of 120 acres. Hyde Park preserves the name. Once cleared the land could be held by the community or sold, but every person benefiting from that land had responsibility for its defence even if his responsibility took the form of defending the walls of the nearest town. In this way towns became independent and formidable communities. When the Normans overran England they often built powerful castles on the outskirts of the larger towns, such as Exeter, to ensure that they did not take their ideas of independence too far.

Towns with fortifications dating from the tenth century may still be found all over Britain. Some have been altered to accommodate later fortifications but many have escaped both that and the even greater danger from vandalistic town planners of the last decade. Two of the earliest to examine are Wallingford and Wareham; the former has substantial remains to the north-west of the town and the latter a rectangular system of earthworks on the north.

As the Normans regarded motte and bailey castles as the most effective way of conquering and holding a country, it is not surprising that little attention was paid to town defences, and these continued on the English pattern of burh bot until the early thirteenth century. During the reigns of William I, William II, Henry I, Matilda, Henry II and Richard I there had been no fear of invasion. But when John became king England faced a double danger. John's strange and vacillating policies made England weak — as was shown by the failures in Normandy and the loss of the formidable Château Gaillard; his erratic policies made it seem that foreign powers might occupy England by invitation. It is now believed that John once contemplated trying to turn England into a Moslem country. Ultimately it was not John but his barons who brought in the foreigners in the form of Prince Louis and his French army, as we saw earlier. The dangers caused by John's policies caused the towns to look anxiously at their defences. The result was a new tax, the murage toll or wall-building tax. This was a levy on goods coming into the town for sale, and although after a time many goods were exempted the revenue was sufficient to provide many of the towns with stone walls. Medieval citizens are often criticized for their narrow streets, rickety houses and insanitary conditions, but the fact that excellent walls were built and maintained suggests considerable skill in civic management.

Towards the end of the Middle Ages, i.e. in the fifteenth century, the collection and allocation of tax money had become extremely complicated and irksome owing to the diversity of goods entering towns. In consequence a different method was introduced, that of taxing property-holders who lived within the town boundaries. They would be the beneficiaries of defence so presumably it was fair for them to pay. Even so, the other method of revenue was never completely abandoned and markets were a useful supplement to a town's finances.

Although the main danger area for invasion is usually

thought to be the south-east, other areas might dispute this. York and Durham had had sufficient experience of invaders from the north to look to their walls; those at York are one of our best reminders of the troubled times of the Middle Ages. Chester was adequately prepared against the dangers of invaders from the north-west; they had come before, they would come again. Carlisle, King's Lynn, Norwich, seem likely enough objectives for attackers but Oxford in the heart of the country much less so; nevertheless Oxford has the remains of substantial town walls and the gates through them. One of the best places from which to see the Oxford wall is New College garden.

When Edward I conquered Wales in the late thirteenth century (they thought of him as an invader: he thought of them as rebels) he was in no doubt about the magnitude of the task of preventing the Welsh from rising against him. To this end he built his chain of great Welsh castles: Conwy, Caernavon, Harlech, Beaumaris, Rhuddlan and Flint, and strengthened many others. Although today the castles themselves are the most easily observable feature of his defensive scheme the town walls were an essential part of it. Today at Conwy it is possible to walk on long sections of the wall, and stand inside some of the bastion towers. It is a revealing experience. There are many reasons for visiting Conwy, its beauty, the castle, the town itself, but none more than the experience of recapturing the feel of being a soldier on a medieval wall-walk.

In the south-east much that was once extremely strong has now disappeared but here, as elsewhere, gates have often been preserved when walls have not. Canterbury, to judge from old prints, must have been a tightly enclosed fortified city. Fortunately portions of the walls and several of the gates remain. They were begun by the Romans and continued till the late Middle Ages, eventually enclosing one hundred acres. The best example of the strength of Canterbury is the West Gate, which dates from 1380 and is still close to its original state.

Although the Roman walls of London have almost entirely disappeared, much of them still exists under the medieval superstructure; however there is a short piece of Roman wall still to be seen in the grounds of the Tower. The size and strength of the later medieval walls can best be appreciated by looking at the section in Cooper's Row, in the City; this is thirty-five feet high and it was probably higher when it was built. The street known as London Wall is slightly misleading for it does not follow the line of the wall but merely joins it. There were seven gates, Aldgate, Ludgate, Aldersgate, Bishopsgate, Newgate, Moorgate and Billingsgate, but nothing remains of them today.

Rochester still has remains of medieval walls but they are not extensive. Rye, which once relied so heavily on its defences and walls, has now lost all but the Landgate. This, however, gives a good idea of the former strength of the town for the gatehouse towers are forty-seven feet high and fifteen feet in diameter. Rye had been attacked and plundered too many times to leave much to chance.

A similar story could be told of Winchelsea, whose misadventures were described earlier in the book. Winchelsea — like Rye an exceptionally beautiful town — is on a hill and covers 150 acres. Here, as at Rye, is a Landgate, a powerful structure well capable of opposing any unwelcome visitors.

Portsmouth's medieval defences have been superseded by later ones, but Southampton has a good section of wall, the Westgate, and the Bargate, which is a miniature castle. Nearly as strong is God's House Gate (fifty-five feet high). Both this and Bargate now contain museums.

Winchester is an interesting example of a town which had to become a fortress because of its history. Militarily Winchester is badly sited but it grew up as a town because it was a convenient market centre, and once in being it needed to be defended. Only two of the original five gates now remain (but there are two castles). The wall enclosed 138 acres. The surviving gates are the Westgate and King's Gate and there is a portion of wall, best seen in the grounds of Wolvesey Castle, which stands up to twenty feet high.

Town walls and battlements were usually furnished with arrow loops and heavily machicolated. Machicolations were projecting shelves of stone with slots in the floor through which red-hot sand, boiling fat, or even arrows could be launched on to an enemy trying to mine or otherwise damage the wall below.

Walled towns, such as we have described here, existed in

many countries, and many are still well preserved, better in fact than they are in this country. The supreme idiocy of the second half of the twentieth century in Britain has been the failure of successive governments to prevent the spoliation of ancient towns, such as Berwick, Oxford, and Cambridge, by tower blocks, multi-storey car parks, and traffic throughways. Within another decade the ubiquitous motor car may no longer have the fuel to probe everywhere and be accommodated to the detriment of the historical heritage. But by then unnecessary motorways and link roads may well have destroyed even more of our heritage. At the moment we have the absurdity of larger faster roads being constructed to take visitors to towns which are rapidly being spoilt in order to meet what inexperienced planners think are the needs of modern living. Already we have nothing to compare with Loches, in France, Bruges in Belgium, or Venice in Italy; soon, unless we take care, we shall have nothing compared even to Calais. In a few years' time the major problem — in the silicon chip age — is going to be that of leisure. Every year several ancient monuments are lost or damaged, sometimes by deliberately careless farmers, sometimes by unrestrained speculators, sometimes by sheer ignorance. Yet the unspoilt countryside and relics of the past are shrines of peace in an age when one of the scarcest and most valuable commodities is tranquillity of mind.

Paradoxically, tranquillity of mind was by no means a permanent condition among our remote ancestors, but that problem was very different. In the earliest period for which one can find a military monument, Crickley Hill in 3000 BC, man's mind was full of doubt about his ability to find food, to endure the winter, and to ward off evil spirits. A thousand years later man built Stonehenge — the gap between the two events is roughly as wide as between us and the Battle of Hastings. The builders of Stonehenge and their predecessors had taken great care over burials but today we do not know what they believed, what their buildings signified, how they were built, nor have we any idea of how they talked, thought or organized themselves. Sometimes the unknown past which we sense when looking at ancient monuments seems sinister though quiescent. We may have a few theories about Stonehenge and

Avebury but what were the menhirs for? Menhirs are single upright stones such as the one nicknamed 'Long Meg' in Cumbria. What did they mean, and what did the Rollright stones mean on Edgehill or the Nine Maidens on Belstone Common or the Rudston monolith? Clearly each of these symbols of antiquity, long barrows, round barrows, menhirs, stone circles, and henges, represents the beliefs of an invader. Their originators were superstitious — but who are we to talk with our lucky charms, our astrologers' columns in the newspapers, and our belief in cult figures? They worshipped strange pagan gods but perhaps their worship gave them more satisfaction than modern man's feverish pursuit of pleasure through the ownership of material goods; cars, houses, furniture, gadgets — many of which give a very poor return for the effort spent in acquiring them.

With the hill forts we feel we are almost in modern times, after all some were built not much over two thousand years ago. But even on a hill fort there is a strange feeling of being far removed from modern life and thought. Their builders and defenders may have been primitive by modern standards of housing, medicine and transport but it is not beyond possibility that a people who could build Maiden Castle or Old Sarum with the resources of the time must have had minds that were as nimble, even though not so well-informed, as our own. In this book we are not concerned with the full range of their minds, fascinating though that would be, but only with their military skills, first as invaders, then as master of anti-invasion techniques. We may be sure that the minds which planned the sophisticated gateways of Iron Age forts planned all sorts of other surprises for the enemies who approached them. It is easy to reach Cissbury Ring today but it must have been a very different matter for a Roman legionary before he began his assault on the fort itself. The Romans eventually captured the hill forts because they had siege engines which could batter down the gatehouses; in this particular they were like men with rifles and guns attacking men with spears. But it is unlikely that a Roman cohort which set off to attack a target arrived with the same number of men it began with. It would have been ambushed a dozen times on the way. The Ancient Britons, it may be remembered, regarded their womenfolk as equals. Boadicea was by no means unique in being a queen and at every level women would take part in the military plan. Women may be smaller than men on average but they can be as enduring and their record as military leaders — when they turn their hands to it — is impressive.

Doubtless the women took their turn on the earthwork defences of the Saxon towns; they certainly took them on the walls of the medieval cities. Cities, in the Middle Ages, needed to be self-reliant. The major problem was to ensure that there were no weak points where walls could be breached or scaled. Even very young children took part in their defence. A heavy stone rolled on to your head by a young child can be just as lethal as one despatched by his father. By all accounts women were the most ferocious of the people defending the walls. Women, knowing that they would certainly be raped, and almost as certainly be killed afterwards, were not disposed either to give in themselves or let the menfolk do so. There would be some apprehension that another part of the wall, which was defended by people of known unreliability, would be letting you down, but in general morale was high. Besiegers of towns who wished to speed up the surrender would sometimes execute hostages, including relations of those watching from the battlements; it availed nothing. Chivalry was usually absent. When the English were besieging Caen in 1417 Sir Edward Springhouse slipped off a scaling ladder and fell into the ditch. The French defenders threw burning straw on to him and roasted him alive.

Of course, not every walled town had to stand siege; some had more than their share, others less. But for a besieged town, such as Carlisle or Berwick, which often had to do battle with the invading Scots; or Rye, Winchelsea or Southampton which had to contend with the French, a siege must have been a time of horror, excitement, terror, elation, and collective morale. There would never be a moment for relaxation until — if they ever did — the attackers withdrew, and even then it might be a ruse. Food must be rationed, and everyone would need to be alert. There are innumerable stories of handsome young men or beautiful young women arriving as traders in a town some months before it was on the invaders' route. Usually they had a good story to tell to justify their stay. Soon

someone would have fallen in love with them and treachery
would be afoot. A girl named Marion de Bruyère unwittingly
betrayed Ludlow Castle in the twelfth century. She let in her
handsome lover by a rope but when they went to her room he
left the rope dangling and a hundred men-at-arms followed
and captured the castle. Today as the visitor leans over the
battlements of wall-walks and looks at people moving peace-
fully on the roads below it may be difficult for him to imagine
such things happening. But happen they did, with disease,
starvation, bloodshed and torture in attendance. Nowadays
cities are sometimes declared as 'open' in the hope that absence
of military installations will save them from attack. The
theory does not find much favour in Coventry or Hiroshima
or Dresden or London. No city, and certainly not those, is ever
separated from the war effort. London came under siege in the
1940s and its citizens displayed a philosophic tenacity which
cannot have been surpassed in the Middle Ages. People picked
their way through smouldering ruins and broken glass to go to
work with 'business as usual'. London charladies, though
warned of the dangers of touching objects dropped from the
air, were always liable to scoop up small incendiary bombs
with a dustpan and brush. Hideous weapons were given amusing nicknames — like 'doodlebugs' — such is morale. A
100-pound bomb landed on No 100 Jermyn Street but did not
explode. A resident took it out of the attic and walked out of
the door carrying it. 'Get a taxi,' he said to a friend. 'I've got a
bomb here and I want to give it some breakfast.' Together
they took it in a taxi and deposited it in a park. He was fined
£100, because it is apparently against the law to walk about
with bombs without official permission.

   With that sort of spirit one feels a man could have defended
an Iron Age fort, a Saxon town, or a medieval city.

6 The Henry VIII Forts

In the sixteenth century it seemed to many that with the development of effective guns the day of the castle and possibly of the walled town was over. However, like many other military forecasts these turned out to be wrong. The walled town, which was developed extensively on the Continent by the predecessors and disciples of Vauban, proved to be one of the most stabilizing factors in the seventeenth and eighteenth centuries, while the castle adapted itself to use the very weapons which were designed to hasten its destruction. Future castles would be designed with oblique surfaces so that shot would glide off them, and there would be a revival of earthworks as soon as it was realized that these were a most effective means of neutralizing cannon shot. Rather surprisingly the old medieval castles were found to have more resistance to the new weapons than had been thought possible. In the English Civil War castles such as Denbigh and Corfe were pounded month after month without much harm coming to the structure. Medieval mortar often proved stronger than the stones it was bonding together. Even more striking examples of the old resisting the new occurred in 1940 when a German Panzer division took a day to blast through the Boulogne medieval town wall, and in 1943 a combined assault by artillery and aerial bomb took four days to overcome the defence of the old palace at Mandalay.

The fortifications which are such an impressive feature of Continental eighteenth-century towns had begun their existence at the end of the fifteenth century. It was found that if walls were strengthened with earthworks the earthwork was comparatively easy to scale. The principle of the moat, which had never been fully abandoned, was now considered more seriously and the new defences generally consisted of an earthwork with a wall supporting the inner side, a deep ditch, another wall on the far side and an earthwork supporting that. Clearly there were various combinations of these methods which could be employed. Cannon could be mounted at the ends of the ditches to fire along them; this would be unfortunate for a body of men crossing at the time for the cannon would be so securely housed that it would be difficult to immobilize. The only disadvantage to the securely housed cannon was that the noise, vibration, and fumes were likely to have a damaging effect on the gunners and the surrounding structure. Nevertheless, even with its obvious disadvantages, this was undoubtedly the correct means of future defence.

Henry VIII, as we noted, had put England in dire peril of invasion from a combined French–Spanish force after 1539. He therefore ordered a chain of coastal forts to extend from Hull to south Wales, although in the event not all of them were built. What was built, however, was an impressive line from Walmer to Pendennis. They are not beautiful but they were no doubt functional enough to please their users. The general pattern was of a central circular structure on the flat summit of which a gun could be mounted to traverse in a complete arc. Below were smaller, semi-circular towers jutting out from the main structure; sometimes there were four, sometimes six. Each point was liberally fitted with protected gun embrasures into which the gun could be withdrawn if required but out of which it could emerge and fire over a wide area; this made the guns more vulnerable but avoided the damage caused by noise, vibration and fumes. The castles tended to be squat and symmetrical in appearance, and more like forts or blockhouses than castles but inside they retained some of the devices of the old concentric design so that an intruder would be isolated in that particular section. Forts of this type had very clear advantages over the ships they opposed. While a ship was clearly silhouetted against the horizon the fort itself made a very poor target with its outline blended into the landscape. In addition a shore fort can always carry heavier guns than most ships, and thus be able to engage its targets at longer ranges. Marksmanship is much less affected than on ship by wind and weather. A fleet which therefore wishes to make headway past a coastal fort is likely to arrange for it to be attacked by a landing party. The World War II film *The Guns of Navarone* is based on this exciting situation. The Henry VIII forts had enough guns of all calibres to deal with everything from bombardment from the sea to land attacks. The only hope of capturing such a fort is usually at night by surprise, in much the same way as some stoutly built medieval castles were made to capitulate by bold men who took advantage of darkness or bad weather.

Many of the Henry VIII castles were adapted to later use. Southsea was captured in a surprise night attack in 1642, at the beginning of the Civil War. It was strengthened in 1814 though the Napoleonic Wars then appeared to be nearly at an end. It was improved again in 1850 when the ambition of Napoleon III seemed to pose a threat, and it was employed in World War I and World War II.

Walmer is one of the smaller castles but is perhaps the most famous because it was officially adopted as the residence of the Warden of the Cinque Ports. It has very fine gardens and parts of the interior are luxurious. Among the more distinguished holders of the post of Warden were William Pitt, the Duke of Wellington and Sir Winston Churchill. Wellington died here in a chair. The boots he made famous are on view and also his extremely narrow bed. When a friend commented on his bed and said it looked too narrow for him to turn over, Wellington replied crisply: 'When it is time to turn over it is time to turn out.'

Deal is larger and considerably more complex than Walmer. Among its refinements is an oven for making cannon shot red-hot before despatching them on to wooden ships. It saw action in 1648 when it was held for the Royalists. A German bomb landed on it in 1941 but only succeeded in damaging some later unwanted additions which have never been replaced.

There were other Henry VIII castles at Sandown (of which little is left), Pendennis, St Mawes (very impressive), St Catherine's (Fowey), Portland, Hurst, Yarmouth, Cowes, Calshot, Camber, Sandgate, Dover (modified), Queenborough, Upnor and Gravesend. St Mawes has an interesting clover-leaf design but when it was called upon for action in the Civil War quickly surrendered on the basis that it could not be defended on the landward side from which the Parliamentarian attack was proceeding. Pendennis, thought to be militarily inferior, held out for six months and only surrendered because one quarter of the garrison was ill and supplies had run out completely.

In peacetime Henry's castles housed small garrisons of twenty to thirty, but in wartime could accommodate up to eight hundred. In addition, smaller blockhouses were built in the Thames estuary, two at Tilbury, two at Gravesend, and one at Higham; these were in the shape of a D.

In the twentieth century all that the Henry VIII castles needed to make them serviceable was a few bags of concrete. However, some were extended — mostly after the main invasion danger had passed.

Effective though the Henry VIII forts were, they were soon to be outmoded by an Italian invention known as the Star fort. In its simplest form this had arrow-head bastions projecting from the centre, but needless to say such fortifications did not stay in simple form for long. The arrow-head bastions permitted converging fire on an attacker, whichever direction he approached from, and he soon realized that he would receive the least fire if he approached the tip of the arrow. This led to the development of the ravelins — low earthworks — from which crossfire could be directed on to an enemy attacking the point of the star. So the process went on with more ravelins, bastions, casemates and a host of other terms such as retrenchments, bermes, caponiers, tenailles and counterguards. The aim of all these improvements was to confuse the attacker and favour the defender but eventually they became such geometrical exercises that it was virtually impossible for the commander to know what was going on. The French brought this type of frontier fort to a high degree of perfection but could not prevent Marlborough slipping by them in the eighteenth-century wars. The best British examples of this type of fortification is at Carisbrooke Castle on the Isle of Wight. Carisbrooke had already been a Roman fort and a Norman castle when in 1597 an Italian engineer added bastioned out works. Berwick too received arrowhead bastions in this period.

The English Civil War, being an internal matter not concerned with invasion, does not require much comment here
but it is worth noting that the science of fortification took
some notable strides forward at this period (1642–51).

The Dutch War of 1665–7, which produced the humiliation
of the Dutch burning Chatham, rang the alarm bells over
coastal defence. Three years after the war was over Charles II
ordered that existing fortifications should be improved and
new ones built; he appointed a Dutchman to organize it. The
latter included Mountbatten Castle and the Citadel at
Plymouth, and Tilbury (which virtually replaced the earlier
fort on the site).

By this time the inhabitants of the walled towns had decided
that the navy was adequate for defence against invaders. It had
proved adequate at the time of the Armada, though less so in
the Dutch wars. The invasion threat of the Seven Years War
had passed off successfully so the future seemed assured. The
situation changed dramatically on the outbreak of the
Napoleonic Wars.

7   The Napoleonic Threats

The news that Napoleon was assembling an invasion fleet at Boulogne in 1803 and was actually preparing to invade England came as a tremendous shock. How great the shock was has already been described; it now remains to describe the physical effects. Not least is the Royal Military Canal. This was dug from Hythe to Rye with the aim of detaching the Dungeness–Romney Marsh area and at the same time making an obstacle which an army would find difficulty in crossing. It was twenty-three miles long, nine feet deep and sixty feet wide. 180 guns had been allotted to provide enfilade fire but by the time the canal was complete (April 1809) fears of invasion were a thing of the past. How much of an impediment it would have been will never be known but experience suggests that a canal of this size would quickly have been bridged or filled in, in places both no doubt.

Other fixed defences were also installed at this period. Sheerness was strengthened and improved and the renowned Martello towers were built. Strictly speaking they should have been named Mortella, for it was the difficulty of capturing a tower of similar design at Cape Mortella in Corsica which caused the design to be adopted for a part of the defences of Britain. Other Martello towers were built in Canada, South Africa and the United States of America, making a total of close on one hundred and fifty. The original tower had been forty feet high, forty-five feet in diameter and with walls thirteen feet thick. The towers built in Britain were from twenty-five to forty feet high, thirty to seventy feet in diameter and with walls approximately eight feet thick. The Martello towers built in Jersey were added to and strengthened by the Germans when they occupied the island in World War II. Martello towers had three storeys: the ground floor contained the magazine and stores, the next floor was for the garrison's living quarters, and the top floor was the gun platform. There are good surviving examples at Eastbourne, Dymchurch, Walton-on-the-Naze, and Felixstowe, but many have now become private houses.

As is the custom, all the defensive installations were allowed to become derelict once the immediate danger had passed, but the 1840s saw a sudden revival of interest in the shore fort. Considerable attention was paid to forts in the Thames estuary which were now renovated and strengthened. However the activities of the 1840s were as nothing to the provisions of the 1860s when a chain of forts was built behind Portsmouth with the intention of preventing the capture of the harbour by French landing parties. Three factors caused the introduction of these expensive additions to national defence. The first was that France under a new Napoleon might wish to avenge Waterloo, the second was that the range of guns had now doubled from 4,000 to 8,000 yards, and the third was that France had superiority in numbers of the new iron warships.

Money spent on defence is usually begrudged until a time of crisis arrives and then those who had been most vociferous in criticizing the previous expenditure are the most vehement in denouncing its inadequacy. The financial provision for the Portsdown forts roused even the most somnolent of the arm-chair strategists from their lethargy and for a while it did seem that there might be some reason for the frenzy which struck Parliament. However in the 1880s there was relief at the presence of the Portsdown forts and in World War II they were found very useful both as air raid shelters and storage dumps. By 1868 five forts had been completed — Purbrook, Widley, Southwick, Nelson and Wallington — and all were obsolete according to the ideas of the time long before the last brick was laid.

The best one to visit is Fort Widley which has recently been repaired to make it safe for visitors. (Not all the forts described here are open to visitors: some are still used by the military.) To the east of the Portsdown forts is the Farlington Redoubt

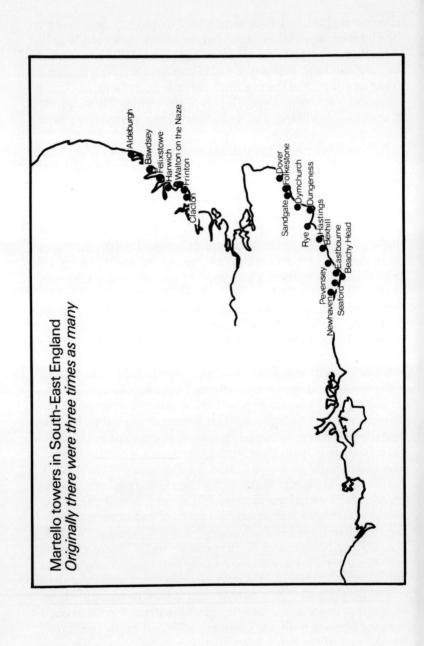

Martello towers in South-East England
Originally there were three times as many

and to the right is Fort Fareham. Another line of forts runs north-south on the west of Gosport: these are forts Elson, Brockhurst, Rowner, Grange and Gomer. Another line was built along the shoreline and (west to east) was Brown Down Battery, Stokes Bay Lines, the Gilkicker Fort, the Lumps Fort and the Eastney Battery. Out in the Solent were the Spitbrook Fort, the Horse Sand Fort, No Man's Land Fort, and St Helen's Fort. Another remarkable fort of this period is the Bovisand Fort at Plymouth.

The 1880s invasion scare produced an elaborate plan for the defence of London but little of its recommendations was put into effect. The defence line was to run from Guildford to Knockholt, near Sevenoaks, then turn north to Dartford. It was to extend into Essex. Fifteen dumps of strategic materials were assembled for use by Volunteer Forces: there is one at Farningham, near Eynsford, Kent, and another at Box Hill, Surrey. But at the turn of the century France was no longer feared as the most likely aggressor; that doubtful honour had fallen to Germany.

During the years between 1900 and the outbreak of World War I the fear of invasion never seems to have been entirely absent. News of the growing power of Germany sent a shiver down the spines of thinking men; fears were not allayed by the publication of several books based on invasion. One was *The Riddle of the Sands* by Erskine Childers (1903); it described the possibilities of a German force landing near the Wash. There were other discourses on the same theme by such eminent writers as 'Saki' (1913), P.G. Wodehouse (1909), and William Le Queux (1910). 'Saki' (H.H. Munro) was well-known as a humorist with a very light touch. His book *When William Came* struck a particularly chilling note for it described England after sudden swift defeat. 'Our ships were good against their ships, our seamen better than their seamen but our ships were not able to cope with their ships plus their superiority in aircraft. Our trained men were good against their trained men but they could not be in several places at once and the enemy could.'

Responsibility for this catastrophic and irreversible defeat was everyone's: 'The government of the day must more or less reflect the ideas and temperament of the nation in all vital matters, and the British nation in those days could not have been persuaded of the deadly nature of its danger — any political party that had said "the danger is enormous and immediate, the sacrifices must be enormous and immediate", would have met with certain defeat at the polls. The working class had a big share of the apathy, and indirectly a greater responsibility, because the voting power was in their hands; their own industrial warfare was more real to them than anything that was threatening from the nation they knew only from samples . . .'

Saki's prophecies were ridiculed. He was killed in 1916 halfway through the war he had prophesied might easily be lost. And of course both World War I and World War II several times came perilously close to being lost.

But neither the warning voices nor the fact that the German officers were reported to drink regular toasts to 'Der Tag' (the opening day of the next war) made much impact on the majority of people and 4th August 1914 came as an enormous surprise to many who were destined to die within the next four years. Even the war itself produced little more effect than the strengthening and extension of existing defences. Guns were mounted along the coastline and forts in the river estuaries — too numerous to mention and mostly inaccessible today — were manned. A new development was the organization of fighter aerodromes at Bekesbourne, Throwley, Detling and Biggin Hill, to protect the capital.

However, in World War I there was little fear of invasion. Admittedly cetain ports were bombarded in surprise attacks. Scarborough, Margate, Broadstairs and even Dover itself were subjected to hit-and-run raids, but these were not preludes to invasion attempts.

World War II saw a very different state of affairs. When the armies had been evacuated from Dunkirk in June 1940 invasion became a very real possibility. In consequence all parts of Britain were alert to invasion by boat or airborne troops and took rapid precautions accordingly. Preparations to repel the potential invader were made in the form of road blocks, pillboxes, beach defences and denial of possible landing grounds. Some of these left no permanent trace but concrete or earthwork defences are still to be seen in many places. Two areas received special attention of which traces may still be seen. One was the Royal Air Force station at Hawkinge, near Folkestone, which had the dubious pleasure of being the nearest airfield to the French coast, the other was Dover Castle, whose subterranean vaults, originally dug out by French prisoners in the Napoleonic Wars, were adapted to be the headquarters of the Flag Officer Commanding Dover. Gunpits were dug for anti-aircraft guns and pill-boxes, i.e. concrete shelters to house guns and their firers, sited on cross-roads and other vital points. Rather more enthusiasm than tactical knowledge was shown in the siting of some of the pill-boxes which today look perfect targets for the German tanks they were meant to check; however all were smothered in camouflage and at the time did not look so exposed. Unfortunately the camouflage around many other obstacles has now disappeared but it included a fairground roundabout, churches, railway stations, haystacks and piles of logs. Some of the pill-boxes subsequently found a use as forage stores, cattle shelters or even houses, proving that a castle may always become a home even if a home is not necessarily a castle. Additions were made to existing fortifications in the shape of dragon's teeth tank-traps around Napoleonic fortifications, and a pill-box for a gun aligned on the bridge by Bodiam Castle. Less satisfactory survivals are abandoned trenches, rotting sandbags, and stretches of rusty barbed wire. Objects found in such areas should not be touched as they may be ingeniously designed bombs, still potential killers.

Pill-boxes, it will be observed, were infinitely varied. There was a standard six-sided pattern, each side being seven feet, as also was the height. The common thickness of walls and roof was fifteen inches and there was usually an internal barrier to protect at least some of the occupants from blast. However, many were not constructed by the Royal Engineers but by local builders, using available materials, and advised by ex-officers from World War I whose experience lay with static rather than mobile warfare. Nevertheless for a defender with a rifle any sort of cover, whether in the form of a ditch or a concrete blockhouse, carries a considerable psychological advantage. Iron Age forts were usually employed for search-light positions, anti-aircraft sites, and observer points. Apparently it was an interesting experience to be on sentry duty at Maiden Castle or Cissbury, surrounded by ghosts of the warriors of over two thousand years.

There are a few other souvenirs of World War II around the beaches of Britain but the best area for seeing what invasion entailed is the French coast. There is a museum at Arromanches but the most impressive testimony of D–Day 1944 is the tangle of wire, gunsites, and trenches which may still be seen on some parts of the coast. On the Cotentin Peninsula it is still possible to see the decaying hulks of invasion barges.

8 Men and Weapons

The art of warfare may be summarized as the art of gaining an advantage which will lead to victory. For the attacker the art will include skill in deploying superior numbers, exploiting surprise, and luring an opponent out of a strong position, but these are only a few of the requirements of a successful attack.

The defender, on the other hand, will endeavour to make the attacker exhaust himself by assaulting strong defences and in that state be vulnerable to counter-attack. But whatever tactics are used, both attacker and defender will rely heavily on weapons to give them an advantage. This was as true in prehistoric times as it is in the age of nuclear weapons and satellites. But it should not be overlooked that although major weapons may establish victory, success can only be confirmed by men carrying personal weapons. In the past, sword and firearm were for long separate weapons; now they are combined to give a soldier a rifle with a bayonet attached.

From the earliest times weapons took two separate and distinct forms: they were held in the hand or they were flung through the air. The first weapon was probably a wooden club, the second a stone which could be thrown.

The club continued in use for thousands of years. In the Middle Ages there were war hammers and maces; both were ideal for cracking plate armour and helmets. There is as much skill in using a club as a weapon as there is in using a tennis racket or cricket bat. Strange, lethal clubs were used in trench warfare in World War I (there are specimens in the Imperial War Museum in Lambeth, London).

The axe was a development of the club and was an enormously popular weapon with the Vikings, who could split their opponents in half with one blow; it was called 'making an eagle'. The battle-axe was used at Hastings by the defeated Saxons and temporarily fell out of favour; however it was soon popular again and became a favourite weapon of Richard Coeur-de-Lion. Battle-axes were huge weapons, requiring great strength and skill to handle but there were also smaller throwing axes of the type that had been used very successfully by the Franks.

The club was adapted to make several other weapons. One was the 'morning star' when it swung a spiked ball held by a short chain. Another was the mace with knobbly projections. This could be used by bishops, who were remarkably warlike in the Middle Ages but whose calling prohibited them from the shedding of blood; it probably did as much damage as a sword. Longer clubs were quickly adapted to jabbing and then to becoming spears with flint heads. Then it was realized that the spear could be thrown. Thus came lances and javelins. With the discovery of bronze, and then iron, spears, swords and axes became more efficient. Various methods were used to project spears further than men could normally throw them. Slings were adapted (aboriginals can sling spears with great power) and then some long-dead genius invented the bow.

The bow began as a small weapon but then took two different forms. One was the crossbow which had become very effective by the twelfth century AD and was drawn by a system of levers or winding; the other was the longbow which became one of the most effective weapons of the Middle Ages. The crossbow projected bolts or quarrels (so called because they had four sides); it had greater length and power than the longbow and did not require strength to use; however it was slow, firing only twice a minute. The longbow, which projected a three-foot arrow (the clothyard shaft) could put twelve arrows into the air per minute and was highly effective at 240 yards, but it required a trained strong man to produce the 70-pound pull required.

Larger weapons were soon developed; these either slung a missile at the target as with the catapult or launched it directly as with a crossbow. The latter form were called ballistas but a whole host of bizarre names grew up as the type of weapon developed. Some were called 'onagers' because their effect was like the kick of a wild ass, others 'mangonels' (from which the word gun was derived), and others petraries. The Romans developed powerful siege artillery with these weapons which had widespread use in the ancient world. After a period of neglect they came into favour again in the Middle Ages and a new one, the trebuchet, was added. The trebuchet was powered by a balanced weight but the other weapons used human hair or horsehair to make elastic ropes. Human hair is more tensile than horsehair and commanded a ready sale. Siege weapons were used to project a variety of missiles, stones, captured spies, dead horses (to spread disease), incendiary material. A substance known as Greek fire which would stick to stone, and burn on water (it must have contained phosphorus), was a terror weapon of the Middle Ages. The secret formula was well-kept; even today we do not know it.

A constant reminder of the former great importance of the profession of smith is shown by the prevalence of the name today. The smith was needed everywhere. He shod horses, made and repaired arrows, sharpened swords and lances, fashioned battle-axes and in addition made the entire range of agricultural implements from ploughs to rakes.

In the early fourteenth century a new weapon gradually came into use — the cannon. It was apparently used at the siege of Metz in 1324 and it is possible it may have been used by the English at the battle of Crécy in 1346, though this seems unlikely. The first cannon were iron tubes made by binding curved iron plates together. The fact that both ends were open meant that breech-loading could be used; it meant however that if the 'shot' of stone or iron was too large the explosion would be more likely to come out of the rear of the gun than the front. There are also several cases on record of the charge exploding inside the gun and blowing the plates out sideways. Usually this killed the crew of 'gynours' as they were called. By the mid-fourteenth century cannon were made of a cast-iron piece of which the middle was bored out. Copper was also used both for the barrel and for the shot. Some highly unsuitable material was used for the shot, and even included pieces of wood. Elevation was made by a series of wedges and the first cannon were by no means as accurate as the old ballistas.

Cannon soon became ridiculously large. There is one preserved at Ghent which was used in 1382: the muzzle is thirty-three inches in diameter and it projected stones weighing up to 600 pounds. An even larger one is at the Tower of London: it was used by the Turks in 1453 and would project a missile up to 1,200 pounds. 'Mons Meg' at Edinburgh Castle is a similar monster. But soon smaller and more practical weapons were in use and these attracted a variety of titles. Cannon became known as ordnance because of the table of ordnances stipulating size, bore, range, etc. On those lists would be found culverins, demi-culverins, sakers, bombards, robinets, etc. but certain guns soon acquired nicknames, such as 'sweet-lips' — used in the Civil War; the great gun used by the Germans to fire at Dover was called 'Big Bertha' after Bertha Krupp.

By the eighteenth century cannon were mobile enough to be used in the field and, as we saw earlier, had a variety of employment on ships. Experiments were conducted with mixed success. Grooving was employed inside the barrel to impart a twist to the shell. New methods were employed to deal with the problem of recoil, of elevation, sighting and laying, of rapid loading and general mobility. Many materials were used in their manufacture: even leather was used in the Civil War. The same type of experimenting went into the projectiles and the charge. Gunpowder is simple enough to make, consisting as it does of saltpetre, sulphur and charcoal, but the problem lies in getting the proportions exactly right and having properly purified saltpetre. It seems doubtful whether gunpowder was invented until the thirteenth century because saltpetre (potassium nitrate) is coarse and impure when mined and not easily purified: it can however be made chemically. The quality and fineness of the sulphur and charcoal can also make a considerable difference to the size and efficiency of the resultant explosion.

In 1845 a new explosive was discovered when cellulose was treated with nitric or sulphuric acid. It was called 'gun-cotton' and manufactured at Faversham in Kent until an explosion wrecked the mills in 1847. The new explosive, although an excellent smokeless propellant, was plagued with problems, causing it to be over volatile. Twenty years later, when it has been mixed with gelatine and rolled into cords, it proved to be reasonably safe and satisfactory. This was nitro-cellulose.

The process was taken a step further by Albert Nobel (subsequently founder of the Nobel Peace Prizes), a Swiss engineer who began to use nitro-glycerine as an explosive for mining in 1859. Nobel stablilized the nitro-glycerine by adding an earth called Kieselguhr. This mixture was named dynamite. Dynamite was subsequently blended with nitro-cellulose and acetone added. The end product was manufactured in cords and became known as 'cordite'. Later developments included lyddite, which acquired its name from the fact of being first tested at Lydd in Kent, TNT which was trinitrotoluene (nitric acid and toluene), and Amatol which was a mixture of TNT and ammonium nitrate. Later developments such as atomic and hydrogen bombs, and rocket propellant fuels are all too familiar to need elaboration here. Students of military history will be aware that rockets are not a novelty but have been used in battle for several hundred years, that is, at least as long as gunpowder. The advantage of a rocket is that it gains rather than loses speed as it approaches the target. A version known as the Congreve rocket (from its inventor) was used in an attack on Boulogne in 1806 with great success; numerous fires were started from ships one and a half miles away. From then on rockets were used considerably and widely. In World War II they were employed as anti-tank weapons (the bazooka) and as guided missiles. Their possibilities, unfortunately, seem to be unlimited.

One of the preoccupations of early artillerymen was to make the projectile as unpleasant as possible when it arrived at its target. The ideal was a combination of shattering explosion and widespread killing power. This was solved by filling the shell with smaller lethal objects which would be scattered as it burst. For this, percussion fuses were required, and duly invented, and the word shrapnel, from the name of the artillery officer who invented 'spherical case shot' in 1813, passed into the language.

The destructive power of nuclear explosives has now developed to the efficiency of absurdity. A few years ago the experts were able to assure us that there were enough explosives in existence to kill the entire population of the world seven times over. Progress must undoubtedly have been made since that assertion and we may be confident, no doubt, that should there be an Armageddon we may all be able to be killed at least ten times over. At the same time it seems a pity that the art of intelligent co-operation has not progressed as fast as the science of explosives and ballistics.

But, of course, it is just as possible to be killed by a small weapon as a large one, and the science of smaller weapons, from the karate chop with a human hand, has not been neglected. The first handguns followed rapidly from the experiments with their larger counterparts. For years they were far less efficient than the longbows they were replacing but their potential had an excellent effect on morale. The problem was to load it and fire without the powder blowing away or getting wet. Most 'hand gonnes' were muzzle-loaded but ignited through a touch hole on top. At first ignition was with a red hot wire but this was soon replaced by 'match' which was cord soaked in saltpetre. Match could burn too fast or too slowly or go out altogether. After a while it was raised or lowered by a trigger — this made the gun a matchlock. Some of these weapons were called hackbuts and others arquebuses. The latter term is often confused with arbalest which is another term for a crossbow. Accuracy was uncertain and reliability poor. Handguns were often heavy and the trigger mechanism, known as the 'lock' from its similarity to doorlocks, was awkward. An even more complicated development was the wheel-lock which had a wheel grating against a piece of yellow pyrites; this produced sparks which ignited the gunpowder in the pan. By the seventeenth century flint was replacing pyrites and produced a reasonably reliable weapon on which the spark was created by the sharp percussion of flint on metal. This method was used very successfully in the 'Brown Bess' musket which was very effective at Waterloo and at other nineteenth-century battles. These were smooth-bored guns but by Waterloo there was already in existence the Baker rifle, a weapon whose barrel was grooved internally (rifled) to cause the bullet to rotate in flight and therefore to fly more accuratley. From these smaller or larger weapons could be produced. Of the many subsequent varieties one of the more famous was the Lee-Enfield. This had originated with the Lee-Metford but it had many well-known predecessors, and many people had contributed to the development of the idea. There was Jacob Snider, a New York inventor who produced a hinged block for the action, an Austrian named von Martini who modified the breach, and an Edinburgh gunsmith called Henry who improved the rifling. Metford was a nineteenth-century English inventor and Lee a Scottish watchmaker. Metford's name disappeared from the rifle when it was improved at the Enfield factory in 1895. This rifle, shortened to become the Short Lee Enfield, was the standard British infantry weapon of World War I. When the Germans invaded France in 1914, the accurate marksmanship of the British soldier, often firing at fifteen rounds a minute, checked the German infantry. So steady and accurate was this fire that it was thought to be automatic. It was not, of course, each shot was ejected by the bolt action which then pushed another into the breach as the action closed. There was an automatic rifle in being as early as 1849 and readers of cowboy fiction will be aware of the popularity of the Winchester repeater. Repeaters, which operated on the principle of harnessing the recoil (at least the blow-back part of it) to reload the gun for the next shot, were excellent weapons when they did not jam. Automatic weapons did not become popular until World War II; the disadvantage is that they use up ammunition very quickly and wastefully. However in the 1970s jamming seems to have become much less frequent and some of the weapons and ammunition lighter. Curiously enough one of the objections to the new designs of rifle was that they were unsuitable for the obsolete drill which armies like to perform as training or on ceremonial occasions. Having adapted themselves to a drill using the NATO SLR (self-loading rifle) drill-masters may shortly have to adapt themselves yet again to a truncated version of it.

In the world of pistols and revolvers the name of Samuel Colt who took out his first patent in 1835 is deservedly famous, but an English gunsmith (Robert Adams) also produced an excellent pistol in 1851. In spite of the feats of legendary heroes, some genuine, some fictional, it is difficult to shoot accurately with a revolver. Thus an automatic which sprays the target with bullets — if it does not jam — is usually but not invariably preferred. Weapons like Lugers and Berettas are much esteemed in fiction. The great controversy over weapons has always been over mobility and hitting power. An automatic pistol is portable but its small-calibre bullet may not stop a determined adversary before that adversary inflicts mortal damage on the firer. A tank needs to be fast enough to get in and out of danger before being hit but it needs armour of adequate strength to protect it if that event occurs. Thus there is an endless rivalry between firepower, speed and protective coating. Likewise aircraft need to be fast enough and manoeuvrable enough to outwit defence but need to carry enough fuel to enable them to stay in the air long enough to be effective.

Aircraft, submarines, and tanks are the means of delivering explosives to the target. The character of weapons has varied little over the years. Grenades, in the form of hand-propelled explosives, have long been with us, mines date back to the beginning of fortification, incendiary material has existed as 'Greek fire' from the earliest times, a form of chemical warfare was practised by poisoning wells and catapulting diseased bodies into towns; even propaganda was foreshadowed by the terrorism which caused resistance to crumble in the ancient world.

Thus the invader with a variety of grenades, an automatic rifle and a bayonet may arrive with a carefully prepared reputation of invincibility; however he may find flame throwers meeting him on the beach and even the water contaminated. *Plus ça change . . .*

9 Communication and Intelligence

One of the greatest problems of commanders up till recent times was transmitting orders to troops and receiving information about the state of the conflict. The battles of Lewes (1264), Edgehill (1642) and Naseby (1645) were all lost because the right wing swept away its opponents and rode off the battlefield. Such examples of failure of communication could be multiplied many hundred times. In ancient times battlefields were not obscured by smoke (though often by dust) and it was not too difficult for a commander, from a suitable viewpoint, to control the opening stages of a battle. Once battle was joined all control could quickly be lost. Even if a commander could see what action was required, his order could miscarry, and even if it arrived could well be misunderstood. The disastrous Charge of the Light Brigade in 1854 was caused because the commander-in-chief was unaware that the target he was indicating was invisible to the brigade to which his order was addressed. In consequence the Light Brigade interpreted the order as best they could — resulting in the destruction of the unit.

Communication posed problems at every stage of a campaign. Who does not recall Lars Porsenna of Clusium and his problems:

> Lars Porsenna of Clusium
> By the nine gods he swore
> That the great House of Tarquin
> Should suffer wrong no more
> By the nine gods he swore it

> And named a trysting day
> And bade his messengers ride forth
> East and west and south and north
> To summon his array

Summoning an array has always been a problem, and to some extent still is. Until comparatively recent times it could be done by messenger, but that messenger would need to have authority if men were to abandon their agricultural pursuits and report with weapons for duty. We cannot but be impressed at the fact that the Ancient Britons mustered some 60,000 defenders to confront the Roman invasion. Clearly there must have been considerable communication across the Channel by which the invasion preparations became known in Britain, and there must have been adequate communication back, for the Romans furnished their ships with artillery with which to break up concentrations of defenders who might mass on the beach to prevent the landing. All this was clearly the result of spies on both sides. There is no doubt however that a widely used method of signalling was by bonfire and smoke. We do not know exactly how the Romans arranged their programmes of smoke signals but we do know that they had a network of signal stations in the Roman Empire and used them regularly. There is no reason to suppose that Europe has systems equivalent to the jungle drums of the primitive African tribes, but it may well be that there were methods of communication which, though not suitable for summoning armies, could convey some forms of news. There are legendary accounts of news travelling faster than the fastest horse in certain Oriental countries; they may, of course, be mere fanciful nonsense but until we know more about telepathy it would be unwise to dismiss them as such.

Leaving on one side the more esoteric means of communication, there is no doubt that the transmission of military messages and intelligence was a major problem over the centuries. The fast runner was a valued figure in the ancient world but his task was not always enviable; sometimes when he brought bad news he could be killed as a reward for his efforts. David, awaiting the news of Absalom's fate, recognized the style of one of his runners from afar. 'He is a good man and he cometh with good tidings,' he said hopefully. But it was not to be.

Beacons, we noted, were used to warn the English of the impending danger of invasion from the Armada in 1588. They were ready for all the subsequent invasion scares until 1940 when one of the more stupid methods of warning was introduced. This was that invasion should be announced by the ringing of church bells, which would otherwise stay silent. The fact that sirens covered the country to warn of air-raids (by the sad undulating sound of 'moaning Minnie') was disregarded. The church bells were chosen, ignoring the fact that churches are not usually on the telephone, that bell-ringing is not a task for an amateur, and that between the alert and the actual ringing of the bells vital time would elapse. They were in fact rung twice, in different areas, on 7th and 9th September, 1940, on false alarms. In April 1943 the order was cancelled and the bells were once more used for their traditional function — the announcement of church services. Today, warning of a national emergency could best be conveyed by television and radio. At peak hours some thirty million people are said to be watching television in Britain and it is reported that there are never less than twelve million listening to radio by day. A good number of people seem to listen to radio during the night too.

The actual movement of troops could not be made without an opponent knowing. There are numerous methods of surveillance of varying degrees of efficiency. The latest is inspection by satellite. But no system of surveillance is going to prevent a surprise attack by modern rocketry. The danger that a misunderstanding could lead to the issuing of a fatal order has been a matter of concern to the nuclear powers for some years. There are disturbing stories of false signals being given before the famous 'hot-line' telephones were installed. Now it is to be hoped that if we are to have mass extermination it will not be by accident.

Control of armies in battle, though much improved today, is still by no means perfect. In World War II there was a special unit with fast light tanks and highly efficient signalling equipment whose function was to report from the forward area to the higher command. It was called 'Phantom'. It was an

excellent idea but the task it attempted verged on the impossible. Once battle is joined there falls over the battlefield what
has aptly been described as 'the fog of war'. Every unit,
whether brigade, regiment, company or platoon, knows the
task. Briefing will have been complete. 'This is where the unit
starts; this is where it finishes. It is all absolutely clear on the
map.'

In the event it becomes rapidly less clear. The start line for
your unit may well be occupied by another formation. This
may be due to an error of command, map-reading, timing or
half a dozen other reasons. So while you cannot be in your
proper place you are blocking somebody else's route. All this
has happened without any assistance from the enemy although
a contribution from that quarter can soon be expected in the
form of bombing or shelling. In certain areas one broken-
down vehicle, perhaps on a crossroads, can cause infinite
confusion till it is removed. Emergency measures taken on the
spot, such as countering an enemy drive to break-through,
must be transmitted to headquarters as they may alter the
general plan. As the battle progresses communication
becomes more difficult, partly because of 'jamming', partly
because of the general confusion. Small wonder that gunners
sometimes shell their own infantry, or fire at their own aircraft, or aircraft bomb their own troops. Up till World War I it
was possible to talk of a 'front line'; now it is no longer
possible to do so and the term 'forward defended localities'
(FDLs) has had to be substituted. But however much the terms
are changed it is unlikely that future wars will avoid the
confusion of firing on their own troops, and misinterpreting
much of the information which comes from the battle area. In
future years military historians, preferably without military
experience, will be able to explain exactly what should have
been done and how. Generals and lesser commanders will be
censored and past battles fought far more efficiently on paper
than ever they could have been at the time.

Though modern large battles produce enormous communication problems, older battles, which were on a much
smaller scale, had no lesser ones. Early battles were usually
decided when one side broke and tried to flee; the greater
number of casualties would occur at this stage, and not be

limited to the eventual losers. The cavalry would usually be the eyes and ears of the commander, but the lack of compasses and watches made the direction and timing of any attack almost impossible. In wooded country it was possible for armies to march right past each other without having a hint of the other's presence. Froissart, the fourteenth-century historian gives a graphic account of English and Scottish armies marching back and forth, cold, wet and hungry, trying to cross flooded rivers, and not being able to find the enemy. Frequently battles took both sides by surprise. Before the Battle of Shrewsbury in 1403 Henry IV was marching his army north with a view to a further campaign against the Scots. Suddenly he learnt that his supporter the Earl of Northumberland had rebelled and was now in league with his former enemy Douglas. The two were planning to join with Glendower and a Welsh army at the strategically important town of Shrewsbury. The fact that Henry was marching north gave him just sufficient time to get to Shrewsbury first. The northern rebels therefore decided there was no alternative but to try their fortunes in battle, which they did, and lost. This was an interesting battle because it made use of deception. Henry dressed up several of his supporters to look like himself, and the rebels found themselves confronted with several kings, not one.

As it was so difficult to obtain an up-to-date picture of the enemy's actions once battle became inevitable, the next best thing was to have a clear idea of his intentions. This brought in the spy and whole world of transmitting secret messages. A spy obviously needs time to work himself into a position where he can obtain information without arousing suspicion. What could be more natural than a Swiss watchmaker acquiring a shop in Scotland in 1923? Being Swiss he would have every reason to conduct a regular correspondence with his relations in Switzerland. The watchmaker in Kirkwall, in the Orkneys, was fond of country walks and bird-watching. In October 1939 the battleship *Royal Oak* was sunk by a torpedo in Scapa Flow. Submarine U47 had found a way in through the nets and defences, and it found its way out again — a feat of great skill and daring. (It was sunk with all hands two years later.) The watchmaker, needless to say, had not been Swiss but German. His name was Von Scheillermann and he had become a British subject, He retired to Germany when his work was done. This type of spy who is working all the time should not be confused with the 'sleeper': the latter has been briefed for a mission but will not be required to take any action until a certain message reaches him. A 'sleeper' is a very worrying type of agent for he never acts at all suspiciously until his time comes. The only protection against the sleeper is to try to ensure that no one working in a sensitive (militarily important) position has anything in his background which might make him a security risk. Thus anyone who has ever been a member of a Communist party organization has a suspicion attached to him that he may still have Communist sympathies although he long since left the organization. People who had been prisoners of war in Korea and who had been subjected to Communist indoctrination were automatically suspect for a long time. The fact that one returned and spied for the Russians while working in British government service did not make life easier for the large number who had treated the attempts at indoctrination with scorn and derision. The case of George Blake shows how difficult it is to know the enemy within. Blake, of Anglo-Dutch parentage, had had an admirable record in British naval intelligence and in 1945 joined the British Foreign Service. He was Vice-Consul in Seoul when the North Koreans captured it. After his release he rejoined the Foreign Service but, until detected, was spying for Russia. In 1961 he was sentenced in a British court to forty-two years' imprisonment but escaped four years later. Blake was such a quiet, unobtrusive person that he was hardly noticed by people who lived or worked near him. In recent years the number of 'defections' between East and West Germany is remarkable; there appears to be an extraordinarily large number of people on both sides who have been trusted with access to material which should clearly have been kept from them; many should not have been employed at all. We might be pardoned for believing that the purpose of labelling material 'secret' etc. is not to make it secure but merely to make it more readily collectable and also able to command a higher price from the enemy.

In general, amateur spies, who defect carrying numbers of

microfilmed documents, are less dangerous than the professional spy. The professional has the military knowledge to judge whether the information he is planning to obtain is of genuine value or not. Such niceties do not concern the amateur who is making a once-for-all defection and there have been cases of amateur spies offering, and even being able to sell, material which has already appeared in technical magazines. The professional, who is often a government employee on a foreign posting (it is astonishing to see the size of some of the Russian embassies), is an adept at putting two and two together and making five.

The methods of spies vary enormously but all have to be painstakingly industrious. They also have to be prepared to work in boring and often uncomfortable situations, A man who works on an incinerator may have access to much valuable information; a woman cleaner has usually an excellent excuse for being almost anywhere. But to do any of the spy's tasks it is necessary to become a different person, a member of the people he is spying on, with a different personality and a different outlook from his normal one. If he were a Scotsman in Russia he would actually have to prefer vodka to whisky. An interesting example of an early spy was King Alfred in the ninth century. He became a strolling musician and as such sat around the camp fire of his enemies the Vikings and entertained them with music and song. Doubtless many of the songs his audience enjoyed most enlarged upon their defeats of the English. Presumably Alfred could sing of those matters with such enthusiasm that he was completely trusted.

Of the spies who passed information about the strength of the defending forces at the time of the Roman and Norman invasions we know nothing — but undoubtedly they were there, reporting numbers, disposition, morale, topography, pathways, and possible food supplies. We know that in the Middle Ages women were frequently used as spies and that when captured their treatment was especially unpleasant. Spies are particularly dangerous and are much hated; their treatment therefore had to be spectacularly unpleasant and it was customary to put a captured spy on to a catapult and launch him back to his own side.

In Tudor times English spying became a professional

though largely internal exercise. During the reign of Henry VII there was always a chance that he might be toppled from the throne on which he sat rather insecurely. From the reign of Henry VIII onwards for several hundred years there was always an undercurrent of plots against the monarch. The first professional spymaster appears to have been Sir Francis Walsingham in the reign of Elizabeth I. Walsingham is believed to be the first man who successfully made a practice of 'turning' spies, that is apprehending them but making them continue to work by sending back a mixture of true and false information. Spies at this time were mainly engaged on organizing plots for internal subversion rather than outside intervention; however it is said that Walsingham knew the date of the Armada.

As weapons improved details of improvements were eagerly sought by competing powers. However information about weapons was not of crucial importance until the atomic bomb was built. It is argued that scientific discoveries must eventually become known but this is hypothesis. When America exploded the first two atomic bombs in 1945 it was a well-kept secret that that was the end of their resources for the time being. Unknown to America and her allies, however, certain scientists closely connected with the project arrived at the conclusion that this deadly secret should be available to all, especially Russia. The result was that invaluable information was passed over by Fuchs, Pontecorvo and others who defected. Fuchs, incidentally, was a refugee from Nazi Germany who had found shelter in Britain; had he decided to try his luck with Russia in the 1930s his story might have been very different.

This type of modern spying differs only in its magnitude from previous activities. There is an extensive dossier on 'master' spies, which includes all those caught; doubtless there is an equally large number of those who remained undetected.

Frederick the Great of Prussia, who could claim to be the founder of the German spy system, recruited them in hundreds. He classified them as four types:

1. Poor people who wished to earn a little money.
2. Double spies — professionals who worked for both sides but who could be used to spread false information unwittingly.

3. High-class spies who would be expensive to hire but who could be very useful.
4. Spies who were blackmailed or otherwise forced into their work.

Today we could add classifications which Frederick could never have dreamed of but which he would have admired. There is the radio-monitoring spy, who not only reads signals not intended for him but also makes deductions from the amount of radio traffic on the air. In World War II most countries were reading enemy codes without suspecting their own had been broken. Tactical moves could be forecast with almost as great an accuracy as if vehicles had been observed moving to battle positions. Of much the same type as the radio monitor is the press monitor. Small items in the news may foreshadow larger events for him. The fact that a well-known footballer, a member of an airborne unit, is now playing in X country tells some interested person that the man's unit has been moved. Someone else no doubt will be able to interpret the purpose of the move. These spies exercise their callings in the most unglamorous and secure ways. However, they know what is being learnt by their employers so they are useful to an enemy who can suborn them. Their corruption is more likely if they are already at odds with society at large, perhaps through an indiscreet love affair, perhaps through homosexuality, perhaps through being in debt. Usually the story is a pitiful one. Occasionally there is a brighter side to the picture. A British embassy employee was discreetly photographed while having an adulterous liaison with a woman from an enemy country. The enemy secret service arranged for him to be interviewed and confronted with the damning evidence of the photographs. Clearly his career and his marriage were both at stake. He picked up the photos one by one, and whistled. 'Jolly good,' he announced after a pause, 'I'll buy six of each.'

Frederick the Great believed that much was to be gained from poor spies. His theories were given ample proof by the activities of Wilhelm Stieber. Before the Austro-Prussian war of 1866 Stieber toured Austria in disguise. His portfolio, so to speak, was wide, for he sold or gave away religious pictures and images to those who appreciated them, and pornographic

pictures and writings to people of the other persuasion. By the
time war broke out Stieber knew more about the Austrian
army and topography than most of the Austrian generals.

But Austria was as nothing to the organization he set up in
France before the Franco–Prussian war of 1870. For this he
used an army of agents, all of whom were accustomed to the
work they did and would therefore not seem out of place. But
railway porters can collect very useful information about railways, barmaids about soldiers, chambermaids about civil ser-
vants, and labourers about supplies. The invasion of France
went like clockwork. The success of Stieber's schemes was so
obvious that after the war had been won there was considerable suspicion attached to German employees in other countries. Stieber was undismayed. He recruited nationals of other
countries, including a number of Swiss. Where Germans were
used it was usually where their presence would attract little
suspicion.

In the early years of the present century the doyen of German spies was Wilhelm Steinhauer. As a young man
Steinhauer had worked for a time in Milwaukee as a cigar
merchant, and then for Pinkerton's Detective Agency. Later
he became bodyguard to the Kaiser and later still Chief of
Intelligence. He travelled widely and was well-liked; occasionally he co-operated with the police forces of other countries in the detection and arrest of criminals. Steinhauer loved
his job and participated actively himself, using, it is said, a
variety of disguises. On one occasion he visited Kirkwall to
have a look at the Grand Fleet but aroused suspicions among
the canny Scots and departed hurriedly. His agents were carefully planted all around southern England, particularly in the
Thames Estuary. One of them was a delightful German professor who spent several of his summer holidays as a paying
guest at a vicarage at Herne Bay. He gave no trouble for he
would cycle off each day to take photographs and make
sketches of the marshes and the birds thereon. The vicar's son,
who later became an officer in the Royal Artillery, used to say
to his father, a most benevolent man who believed ill of no
one: 'Look, this fellow must be a spy. Look at the way he goes
on.' 'A spy. Oh, no my dear boy, I'm sure he couldn't be.' So,
in spite of the son's efforts, the professor continued to enjoy

his holidays right up till 1914. A rather less successful agent was one Frederick Schroeder (otherwise Gould). Schroeder had bought a pub in Chatham, but feeling that he had perhaps aroused suspicion sold it and moved to London. The new landlord at Chatham was astonished to find the attic of the pub full of documents, plans and correspondence. Schroeder was subsequently arrested on a train at Charing Cross en route to Berlin.

Double spies are usually known to both sides but are considered to be too useful to be removed. A double spy who is careful may continue to work for both sides on a lucrative basis but has the interesting thought at the back of his mind that at any moment he might appear to have outlived his usefulness to one side or the other. In those circumstances he would do well to retire swiftly and unobtrusively to an enormous distance.

Frederick's third category of high-class spies who could be bought at a high price would usually be people who are characterized by what is known in modern jargon as 'a character defect', The greedy, the ambitious, the unsuccessful gamblers, the vain, could all be potential recruits. They would be useful but the very characteristic which had made them spies in the first place would make them untrustworthy — a fact which would not have passed unnoticed by their new paymasters. Almost equally unreliable for more than short-term assignments would be those who had been blackmailed or otherwise coerced into spying. Such spies could be stricken with remorse and confess all. They might even become dangerous double-agents. But they could be useful just before an invasion.

The most famous, but not necessarily the most important spy was undoubtedly Mata Hari. She was Dutch and married a Dutchman with the surprising name of MacLeod. A distant ancestor of this Dutch officer had been a Scot but he was no credit to his name for he drank excessively and beat her. Eventually she left him and went to Paris where she went on the stage (without previous experience) and was a great success. She was an even greater success without her clothes in private salons and became what today would be described as an eminently successful call-girl. There was no need for her to become a spy for she was already making large sums of money but none the less she was recruited into the German service and made even more. When she realized she had aroused suspicion she offered to spy for France against Germany but this did not save her from a French firing squad in 1917. Mata Hari was flamboyant, irrational, but very brave. She was also very attractive and a good actress, and all in all, probably deserves her fame as the most renowned of women spies.

Old-fashioned spies appear to have been motivated by patriotism or desire for gain, for the most part. After World War I a new category of spy had to be reckoned with: this was the ideological spy.

The carnage of World War I was so appalling that many people wondered what could be done to avoid a repetition of such horror in the future. The causes of World War I, or indeed of any war, are much more complex than is generally appreciated. It may, of course, be perfectly reasonable to affirm that wars are caused by capitalism and the rivalry for markets; the fact that after World War I the world was bedevilled by economic booms and slumps, and Germany, which had been deprived of its colonial outlets, was agitating for their return, appeared to confirm this view of the cause of wars. Subsequent experience of economics suggests that this subject, on which there are so many experts, is one of the least understood. However, there were many who believed that the Russian revolution of 1917 had shown the way to the abolition of evils caused by economic factors and if that revolution could spread over the rest of the world an earthly paradise would arrive. The fact that neither Russia nor her imitators had much success in the economic field and rather less in creating a terrestrial paradise was glossed over by her admirers who believed that once Communism was world-wide a new and happier era would dawn. This led to a fresh type of spy who worked, often with little or no pay, for that objective. It seems to have been believed that if the military secrets of the West (all countries have special knowledge which they do not wish others to know) were betrayed to the Russians, the Soviet Union would the more easily be able to spread its doctrine over the world. Spies who worked in this field were not usually in any military employment but because of their excellent academic records were usually in high-level diplomatic, administrative or intelligence work. Three notorious British spies were Philby, MacLean and Burgess. It has been said that the beginning of their Communist affiliation began in Cambridge in the 1930s. From this it has been alleged that most of Cambridge was Communist in the period. This is pure nonsense. The majority of the undergraduates at Cambridge were not interested in politics; the problems of games, work and finding a girl in a highly competitive environment occupied all their time and thought. But if five people had wished to form a debating club to discuss 'The Value of Murder and Anarchy', or 'The Merits and Social Decline of the Penny-Farthing Bicycle', this would have been perfectly possible and attracted no notice at all, however much they courted it. Considerable misunderstanding has been created by the prominence given in the press to the University Unions (Debating Societies). A mere fraction of undergraduates become members but because the Unions offer a stepping stone to a political career their antics attract attention outside the universities. Within, most undergraduates do not merely not care what the Unions debate, they do not even bother to know. The 1929 Oxford Union Debate that 'This House will not fight for King and Country' was originally a light-hearted, irresponsible joke.

But in any society there are certain to be people who are both politically motivated and active. Some miners were merely interested in a pint of beer and pigeon-fancying; others would read Marx and bicycle around in the early morning delivering copies of the *Daily Worker* (now *Morning Star*) to their comrades.

As military matters became more complicated and advanced and as nations moved into the lunatic world of competing with weapons of mass destruction, there was a universal fear that a rival might suddenly discover the ultimate weapon. First it was the atom bomb, then the hydrogen bomb, then the rocket, then the satellite — thus to the death ray, the killer satellite, nerve gases and so on. Satellites orbiting made it very difficult for a country to make military preparations without some knowledge of this event reaching their rivals. But there was another problem. Sometimes an employee would genuinely fall in love and betray his or her country in order to be with the lover on the other side of the Iron Curtain. NATO countries are particularly vulnerable to spies operating in their installations as there were so many nationalities involved, and so many uniforms. (It is said that in the middle of World War II an actor walked about London all day in a German uniform which had been made for a stage production; all the notice he ever attracted was a few salutes.)

The Communist countries were vulnerable in a different way. The reasons for defecting could be many. Money might be a factor but a more usual one was the 'glamour' of life in the West.

A new type of defector-spy seemed to have appeared in March 1979. This was Miss Ursel Lorenzen, a senior secretary working for the Director of NATO Council operations. She had been a secretary for twelve years but, in her interview on East German television after defecting, she said she had departed (taking top secret details of the latest NATO plans) because she felt that if the West were attacked NATO's counter-thrust would destroy much of north-eastern Germany. As a German she felt this could not be tolerated.

Purists might feel that this reasoning held fallacies. If the Russians did not attack there would be no counter-stroke. To hand over to the Russians plans which might give them a temporary advantage and make them feel in a stronger position to attack (and thus bring about the counter-stroke) would hardly seem to be in the best interests of her native country. But if in fact the reason happens to be true, it creates a new category of spy — one who, however illogical, believes she is preventing rather than assisting war.

Damaging though individual spies can be, their present-day importance is overshadowed by the machine. Radio and satellite surveillance have already been mentioned. One of the most astonishing stories of World War II was the Ultra system. Ultra was the name given to the operation by which the Allies used a German encoding machine of infinite complexity (named the Enigma machine) to decipher intercepted German messages. Thus the Allies knew most, though not all, of the German intentions throughout the war. They knew of the German plan to invade Russia in 1941 from several sources, and warned Stalin but he refused to believe the warnings.

(There was, of course, no reason why we should warn Stalin; the Russians were loosely allied to the Germans against whom we were fighting for our lives.) But knowing the German intentions did not invariably mean we could frustrate them. A champion boxer may announce his intention of giving you a punch on the nose but if you have no resources to deal with this situation the foreknowledge will avail you little. Enormously valuable though the Enigma knowledge was, there were occasions when it did not arrive in time for it to be acted on, and on occasion the information it gave was misinterpreted. In the critical battle of Alamein in October 1942 Ultra could not handle the intercepts quickly enough to make a significant difference to the decisions; most of the deductions necessary for winning the battle had already been made by General Montgomery and added to the information he had previously received from Ultra. On the other hand, when the German battleship *Tirpitz* appeared to be venturing out to attack convoy PQ17 in July 1942 a disastrous order to scatter had been given to the convoy, most of which was then sunk. Ultra had understood the original order but not the reservations to it, with the result that an event which did not occur was anticipated and this led to an erroneous decision.

Apart from an occasional lapse, such as these, the value of Ultra was virtually unlimited. One of the most astonishing aspects of it was the way in which the secret was kept, not merely from our enemies but also from ourselves. Large numbers of people worked on Ultra but did not know of the participation of the others until 1974 when permission was given for the secret to be let out. Whether it is in the Western interest for wartime secrets to be divulged so freely is debatable. The assumption is that potential enemies must already know such secrets; this is by no means true. At the moment of writing (March 1979) an American journal is trying to publish the secrets of the manufacture of the hydrogen bomb. If it succeeds in defying the authority of the United States Government, the journal should achieve a useful sale among terrorist organizations and the less stable dictatorships.

There is a curious contrast between the attitudes of state and people to spies and traitors in peacetime and wartime. William Joyce (nicknamed Lord Haw-Haw) was executed for making

broadcasts on behalf of the Nazis. As he had once taken an oath
of allegiance as a member of the London University OTC, his
claim that he was Irish, American, and even a naturalized
German, failed to save him. Such was wartime feeling: in
peacetime he would probably have been regarded as a brilliant
actor and recommended for an OBE.

Spies and traitors receive short shrift in wartime and it is
rash to be suspected of being either. When Britain was under
the threat of invasion and being bombed nightly it was essential to have a complete black-out. No light must emerge from
a building at night. This meant heavy curtains around doors
and windows, blacking out skylights, diminishing car lights,
not allowing torches to flash upwards, and generally living in
very stuffy and claustrophobic conditions. A badly 'blacked-
out' window which allowed a pencil of light to escape would
be reported by a passer-by — if not already seen by an air raid
warden — and the offender would be heavily fined. People
using torches in coastal areas to walk home at night were often
under suspicion of signalling to submarines or aircraft. Some
imagination is needed to assess the value of a torch flashing to a
half-submerged submarine or an aircraft already dodging
searchlights and anti-aircraft fire. It was said that the glow on
the end of a cigarette could be seen from 30,000 feet, so
smoking in the dark, particularly of pipes, was discouraged.
Magistrates were as zealous as the ARP wardens. A Swansea
man was fined £20 for striking a match in the street at night.
His excuse was that he had dropped his false teeth and had had
to strike a match to look for them. His plea was not accepted.

One might wonder what sort of message could be conveyed
to an aircraft by a shaded match at street level, particularly as
the Mumbles lighthouse sent out a rather stronger light just off
the nearby coast.

But it should not be forgotten that there was a widespread
fear that a super bomb, containing gas perhaps, might be
dropped on to the middle of a city and wipe out most of its
inhabitants. Indeed, later in the war super bombs did just that
to Hiroshima and Nagasaki. Apprehension about gas was
widespread and it was not allayed by Government insistence
that everyone should have a gas mask, and be forced to carry it
if a member of the Services (where it was called a 'respirator

anti-gas'). The origins of most of this dismay are to be found in the pre-war writings of various scientific 'experts'. They included Professor J.B.S. Haldane, an old Etonian Communist. Haldane was a brilliant biochemist and a fluent writer; for some years he was editor of the Communist *Daily Worker*. Writers of Haldane's persuasion used to assert that one bomb would kill an average of 50,000 people in a city; he cannot have believed it himself but it gave great encouragement to left-wing pacifists or appeasement advocates.

In peacetime it is easy to take a philosophic view of spying or propaganda in the service of the enemy, of swindling on defence contracts, of laxness in preserving vital military secrets. In wartime a slightly sterner view is taken, particularly by the serviceman who is in danger of being killed (and often is) because someone's greed, stupidity or incompetence has ensured that his enemy knows all about his weapons, his plans, and has perhaps traded away assets vital to his security. It may be folly to have allowed vital bases such as Aden, Malta, the Seychelles (there were many) to be handed over to demagogues claiming to represent the will of the inhabitants. Aden is the principal port of the People's Democratic Republic of Yemen. It was given independence by Britain in 1967, and aid to set it on its democratic path. Subsequently it has become firmly aligned in the Soviet camp, is host to a number of Cuban soldiers, and in March 1979 invaded the North Yemen (Yemen Arab Republic) which is not in the Soviet bloc — so far. Democracy in South Yemen is now limited to the mention of the word in its name but neither the present state of the country nor its policy towards its neighbour came as a surprise to anyone who had the faintest understanding of this strategic area. History may perhaps decide that the folly of the Aden policy was tantamount to treachery. And Malta? And Rhodesia?

A cheerful indifference to our menacing military and economic weakness could perhaps be overlooked in those liberal thinkers who believe that the Warsaw Pact army, navy and air force are just for fun and not designed to hurt anyone, but it is difficult to understand their indifference to the state of some of the peoples who have been released from colonial rule. Vietnam became a symbol of reproach to the Americans who tried to preserve a more democratic system than the present one. Vietnam has subsequently invaded her neighbour Cambodia, whose régime was certainly the most brutal and repressive since the Mongols (but without stirring any Western liberal consciences), and Vietnam has herself been invaded by China. Who is to be blamed for the misery in this area? Or in Amin's Uganda? Or in a number of other countries? The answer is those who encouraged the granting of self-government before countries were ready for it, and took insufficient precautions against its abuse, and of course the Soviet bloc for supplying arms and subversive agents. So here in the West we have a new form of traitor, the ideologist who believes so firmly in an outmoded theory that he pushes it forward at all costs and in spite of overwhelming evidence that the system he is introducing is, in its present form, a short cut to disaster.

One of the reasons why spies and traitors, whether they work for cash or ideology, are successful is because most people do not want to know what is going on if it is likely to involve them in trouble. When the enemy is at the gate, as he was in 1940, matters took a very different turn. But not always. One of the most revealing discoveries of World War II was that while most of the population is prepared to take great risks, to be unselfish, cheerful, and do their utmost in the battle for survival, there are some who, though perhaps not intending to assist the enemy, by their actions contribute to doing so. A sobering thought to many was that in 1941, when a 'Tanks for Russia' week was organized, production was higher than it was for our own forces. Russia was indeed an ally but our own forces included our own kith and kin. One of the best-kept secrets of the war was the strike by Southampton dockers who refused to handle the tanks for a cavalry regiment just after D-Day because one had slipped out of its holder and crashed on to a deck. The fact that the men in those tanks were ready to sacrifice their lives for their country did not prevent the dockers delaying the loading by four days and doubtless therefore causing many casualties among our own troops who were relying on the arrival of that regiment. There were extraordinary incidents at Liverpool too where vital ship repairs were delayed deliberately. The modern word for the perpetrators of such acts is 'mindless' but whatever they are called they are as dangerous as the actions of the enemy, sometimes more so.

A more heartening aspect of World War II experience is the way many spies were caught and 'turned', a process which is described more fully later. Some of the early spies were extraordinarily amateurish. They included a Dutchman who landed in the early hours of the morning and made his way to a local pub where he asked to buy cider. The landlady kindly explained that the pub would not be open till ten, but suggested he should fill in his time by having a look at the very interesting local church and come back at the hour of opening. He did this, but in the meantime the landlady, suspecting that this lack of familiarity with the licensing laws was at least unusual, had arranged for the police to meet him. He was executed shortly afterwards.

One of the more resourceful spies managed to get himself a job in the Post Office and thence a move to the Censorship Department in World War I. Any titbits which came his way by means of executing his usual duties he was able to send overseas in an envelope franked 'Passed by the Censor'.

He at least had found a secure method of transmitting his messages. Others were less lucky and usually had to resort to codes. Most spies are caught through the means used to transmit their messages: actually obtaining the information may lead to suspicion; passing it leads to proof.

The world of code messages, as might be expected, is bizarre. Codes have been used since ancient time but the process of communication has quickened up considerably since a messenger had his head shaved, had a message tattooed on it and then grew his hair over it. The recipient then shaved off the man's hair and read the message. This method was used to pass a secret message from Persia to Greece.

The science of codes and ciphers is called cryptography and derives from the Greek *kryptos* (secret) and *graphos* (writing). It includes cipher, which is a corruption of the Hebraic *saphar* (number), but the difference between the two is that a cipher reproduces each letter of the original, whereas a code need not. Thus a simple cipher for 'apple' could be made by merely writing it with the following letter in the alphabet for each letter in the original. Thus it could become 'bqqmf', or be in numbers, or part letters and part numbers. However 'apple' could also be conveyed by a different word such as 'ru' but for this the recipient would need a code book to cover all the words likely to be used. A flag is a code in that it symbolizes something else. Naval signalling owes much to Admiral Kempenfelt in the eighteenth century for he devised a system of using coloured flags with numbers to convey the comparatively simple orders needed for naval manoeuvres. A system of dots and dashes makes the morse code, although this is less a code than a form of communication.

Needless to say all the basic systems are so simple to a professional cryptographer that he can unravel them in seconds. Considerably more difficult are agreed messages of the type which were sent over the radio to our agents in occupied countries during World War II. Usually these were mixed up with scores of meaningless messages which could vary from 'lonely heart' greetings — 'Muriel is wearing David's bedsocks every night in love for him' — to news about coffee crops in Brazil. The warning code for the imminence of D–Day was by the opening lines of Verlaine's poem to the Autumn. Messages of this nature would usually be broadcast on the Overseas Service of the BBC after the main news of the day. It was a strange experience for a citizen who had just settled into the air raid shelter for the night, in a city such as Bristol or Birmingham, to hear these strange mysterious messages going out to agents in remote and dangerous situations. They were also heard by German monitoring services who spared no effort to break the code. Such messages are somewhat vulnerable because (a) the agent might be prevented from listening at the critical time and (b) a repetition could give rise to the suspicion that something important was being communicated.

Mechanical enciphering and decoding has, of course, been completely changed by the computer, and in the process lost any romance that might otherwise be attached to the procedure of enciphering and decoding. However, simple codes will never be completely outmoded even though their use can sometimes lead to disasters. Just before the Gunpowder Treason of 1605, when Guy Fawkes and others planned to blow up the Houses of Parliament, one of the conspirators sent a message to his cousin begging him not to attend Parliament on the 5th November 'on account of a great blow which is impending'. The recipient sent the letter to James I, who then ordered the cellars to be searched. Guy Fawkes was discovered with a huge hoard of gunpowder all ready to produce the 'great blow'.

Other means of passing warnings were more subtle. One was to wind a tape around and along a stick and then print a message on it. The tape would then be unwound and appear merely to be decorated with a series of random letters. However, the recipient would know the exact diameter of the stick around which it should be wound for decoding and have a replica. A code of this nature passed a message in 406 BC to Lysander of Sparta and caused him to make a pre-emptive strike against his enemies.

An extremely simple code to decipher — although it may require some ingenuity on the part of the sender — is the letter which contains a different message from the one it appears to convey. By the simple process of merely reading every fifth letter (or word) a totally different message appears. A more complicated version of the same process is to have a pre-arranged grille in the hands of the recipient. The grille is simply a piece of paper with holes in it. Placed over a letter it will show the words which are under the holes.

One of the problems with codes is that they can easily set the cryptographer on the path of fantasy. For long it has been suspected that William Shakespeare was too uneducated to write the plays attributed to him. But, if so, who could have written them? This little problem could easily be solved by a cryptographer who would assume that, although the true author might wish to remain anonymous in his lifetime he would like the cryptographers of posterity to announce his identity. The fact that Francis Bacon, the Lord Chancellor and essayist, was interested in cryptography supplied the necessary answer for one enthusiast. A little proof would help and this was quickly found in the inscription on Shakespeare's tomb which begins:

> Good friend for Jesus' sake forebeare
> To digg the dust encloased heare.

This was what is known as a tri-lateral cipher, rather too

lengthy to be analysed here, but proof enough for those who wished it!

The code book was not invented until 1776. Its inventor was an American, Arthur Lee, but it was not used officially until 1789. The code book may be a special book or any book, provided it is a standard edition. Thus a message could be sent to the holder of Daniel Defoe's *Robinson Crusoe*. A series of numbers could set him decoding from previously arranged pages, e.g. 221. Perhaps 3, 6, 8, 19, 22, 31, etc. would convey all that was needed.

One advantage of basic codes — which can partly offset the ease with which they can be broken — is that their simplicity leads to fewer mistakes. One of the revelations of World War II was the amount of delay on urgent messages which could be caused by minor enciphering mistakes. General A gives a message to the encipherer who then passes it to Signals. A mistake could be made by the encipherer, or by the person transmitting through the signals system, or by the receiver. The message would then be deciphered. The addressee finds part (or all) of the message incomprehensible. So a check on the message is requested (which takes time on circuits which are already probably overloaded). The message is then repeated, correctly this time, In all, the message, full of urgent, top secret orders, has taken twice as much time as it should have done.

Simple code names produced some peculiar situations in the early days of World War II when armies frequently moved rapidly, as in France, the desert, and the Far East. Units were given simple code names which were brief and secret. It was obviously more convenient to transmit a message from 'Wexo' to 'Rupo' using four-letter codes than to keep repeating from Headquarters 3rd Infantry Division to No. 3 Independent Reconnaissance Company. However, if a unit was overrun and had its code books captured — an easy occurrence in mobile warfare — the entire code system needed to be changed. This would be no great problem, for all that would be necessary would be for Headquarters to authorize a change to the next code in sequence. Assuming that the first code was A, by the third week of a campaign the codes might have moved up as far as D.

Among the new code words many of the old ones would reappear — this time referring to different units. Thus HQ 3 Infantry Division might now be Tiko and No. 3 Reconnaissance Company now Polo. However, if the warfare was exceptionally fluid some units might not have received the notification of the change to the new code and still be working on the old one. This could lead to considerable surprise and dismay, not to say confusion. Thus No. 3 Commando, formerly Hopo, could receive a message intended for the new Hopo, which might be a Field Laundry Unit: 'Collect and disinfest all laundry in your district.' On the other hand, No. 322 Field Laundry Unit, with a strength of ten men, might receive a message: 'Attack the Japanese 1st Guards Battalion which is now entering your area.' This is a somewhat simplified version of events which occasionally occurred.

Code names were used for invasions, and became famous in their own right: the German invasion of Russia was 'Barbarossa'; Hitler's projected invasion of Britain in 1940 was 'Sealion'; the Allied invasion of France was 'Overlord'. Beaches were given code names such as 'Juno', 'Gold', 'Utah' and 'Omaha'; the artificial harbour was 'Mulberry'; and the pipeline under the ocean easily became 'Pluto'. However, the Arnhem operation, 'Market Garden', had little that was humorous about it.

Other well-known code names were Operation 'Husky' for the Sicily landings and 'Torch' for the landing of 1st Army in Africa. 'Zipper' was the name chosen for the return invasion of Malaya along the west coast in 1945. The war was over before it took place but eventually it was carried through as an exercise to assess how it would have gone had it been necessary in the later stages of the war.

Code names were given to spies and agents. 'Cicero' was an Albanian who became valet to the British Ambassador in Turkey in 1943. He opened the Embassy safe and photographed confidential papers and ciphers. He offered the photos to the Germans and after some doubts on their part was paid handsomely. However the Abwehr (German Secret Service) thought that information so easily obtained must be 'planted' and much of it was not believed. The notes used to pay 'Cicero' were mostly German forgeries of Bank of England notes.

Code names have not diminished since the end of World War II but have been carried on by the services and also frequently introduced into civilian life. In 1946 the Services made great efforts to give a few days' home leave to troops serving overseas in the Mediterranean area. This was largely at the instigation of the wives and was dubbed (officially) Operation 'Henpeck'. Subsequently code words have appeared in all sorts of guises in civilian life, accompanied by other martial terms such as export 'target', 'an all-out offensive against poverty', 'three-pronged attacks on inefficiency', etc. The motor industry has been particularly prone to using such expressions.

Military terminology seems to proliferate in relation to the length of time which has elapsed since it was needed. Even in the Services many terms are used without anyone giving a thought to the humorous flavour they once had. For example, commander-in-chief is 'Sunray', although this is not always a fair description of his aspect. An abbreviation sometimes becomes a code word. Thus a 'Snafu' was originally the cynical abbreviation 'Situation normal — all fouled up'. Soldiers tend to develop their own interpretation of words which are abbreviations. Thus in wartime NAAFI, the 'Naffy' which is the Navy, Army and Air Force Institute and runs shops in barracks, was said to mean 'No Aim, Ambition or F—ing Interest'. The Naffy today, we hasten to add, is a very different matter.

But even in wartime codes acquired a bizarre humour. In mobile warfare there was often no time to adopt a proper system of code and therefore some commanders derived their own coded versions of what they felt was essential security. There were occasions when commanders of tank forces needed to give instructions but obviously did not wish the enemy to understand them. They therefore adopted their own private coding. One battalion commander in the Western Desert conveyed his orders by reference to an eighteenth-century battle with which he, as a student of military history, was familiar but which was pure mystery to his subordinates. Field-Marshal Montgomery took apparent pleasure in talking of 'hitting the enemy for six'. The expression was, of course, perfectly intelligible to English listeners and to people from the Commonwealth but mystified and often annoyed Americans. Analogies from baseball would no doubt have been equally baffling to the English.

In general it was in idiomatic expressions that Germans and Italians found their greatest problems. A spy, hearing an idiomatic expression would feel he *ought* to understand it and would attempt to prove he did. A person with nothing to conceal would shrug off the fact that he did not fully understand a sentence in which an unfamiliar idiom was used. Misuse of an idiom could be fatal. A German saying 'I know damn all about love' might imagine he was making an affirmative statement and not a negative one.

Before World War II the BBC did not name its news readers, although their voices became familiar enough. However, during the war it was felt that there might be circumstances in which the regular transmissions were interrupted and the enemy might try to fill the gap, using, of course, a lot of false information. News readers were therefore named and the very sound of their voices gave an impression of confidence and continuity. If London had been heavily blitzed overnight it was no mean comfort to hear the familiar voice of, say, Alvar Liddell, calmly reading the morning news as if nothing had happened. Of course, the broadcast could have been made even if London had been bombed flat but those not living nearby would not know it, and their morale would not be affected. Morale was, of course, of enormous importance. Regular broadcasts by Churchill, honesty in the admission of mistakes and of making claims, familiar voices and humour, all contributed to the fighting, enduring spirit of the nation. Information about the national morale is therefore eagerly sought by intelligence sources, as is also information about the effect on it of disconcerting propaganda stories. Had Hitler thought British morale was low in 1940 he might have staked everything on invasion, whether he had control of the air or not. However, although German propaganda made great efforts to spread the belief that British morale was at the point of crumbling in World War II the view was treated with derision.

Over all, morale in Britain was astonishingly high. There were, of course, times and places when after a series of heavy air raids, official opinion was concerned, but the fact that Hitler, Goering, Goebbels and Mussolini were seen as slightly comic figures was a better factor for morale than believing them to be as nasty as they undoubtedly were. The feeling that everyone was in it together, that the rationing situation was fairly worked out and administered, undoubtedly produced a feeling of solidarity under the endless and dreary sequence of bombing, death and shortages. Queueing for everything was undoubtedly one of the greater strains — waiting for an hour for a pound of indifferent tomatoes or two or three buns. Tea, which was rationed, was the great restorative when alcoholic drinks virtually disappeared. Saved from death and muti-lation, confronted with the death of a close relative, losing the treasured possessions of a lifetime — the immediate remedy for these was a cup of tea and — if lucky — a cigarette.

It was easier for enemy agents to convey to their intelligence services the importance of cigarettes in wartime that it is to convey the same thought to the present situation. Nobody ever thought that cigarettes might be harmful, apart from making the smoker cough. However, for a person being bombed night after night — and often in the day too — the thought of a cigarette causing lung cancer in the distant future would have been the least of his worries. Cigarettes, of course, are a hazard. They may be dropped and start fires, they may be observed by the enemy at a distance and illuminate a target, they are messy, unhygienic and expensive. All this is so but without cigarettes national morale — in any country — might have been hard to maintain. Perhaps the poets who wrote so enthusiastically of the pleasure of smoking knew more than our disease statistics. This, incidentally, is being written by a non-smoker but one who in wartime knew the pleasure of relaxing tension with a cigarette.

One of the greatest Allied successes of World War II was what became known as the Double Cross system. This was a British operation by which the XX Committee, under the Chairmanship of Sir John Masterman effectively turned the majority of the German spies sent to this country between 1939 and 1945. This enabled us to mount one of the most extraordinary deception campaigns in the history of warfare. When 'turned', the foreign spy continued to work for his former masters, and supplied much apparently useful information. But with it he would supply other false information which could not be checked easily.

One result of Double Cross was that the Allies were able to keep the Germans out of certain sea areas on the false information that they were very heavily mined. Another deception was concerned with the opening of the Second Front. A completely false army was to be observed in the Dover area, complete even to an impersonation of Field-Marshal Montgomery. Much of this army was the creation of a series of signals to different (imaginary) formations within it, although there were more physical objects, such as dummy tanks and barges, as well. This resulted in the firm German conviction that the main landing would be in the Calais area. So strongly was this belief held by the German High Command that even after the main invasion had taken place further west a strong German army was in readiness for another Allied landing near Calais. The fact that the landing in the Pas de Calais never took place was explained by the Germans — to themselves — as being due to the unexpected success of the other landings.

Deception was maintained throughout World War II but not without anxiety and difficulty. Sir John Masterman considered that had the D-Day landings not been able to take place in June 1944 the whole of the 'turned' spy operation known as Double Cross would probably have been discovered by the Germans. As it was, there were many difficult moments when the Committee was not sure whether one of the 'doubles' had turned again. The story of the double spies is one of the most extraordinary of the war. They were given somewhat bizarre code names: 'Tricycle', 'Biscuit', 'Celery', 'Lipstick'. All the spies sent by the Germans were given briefings and long questionnaires to complete. Some were required to send in the answers by wireless, others by secret writing. In order to preserve the illusion that they were still spying for Germany, and had not been captured and turned, it was necessary for them to send off a considerable quantity of information; at the same time this would have to be the sort of information a spy could have obtained in the course of his work. To have given the spy information he could not have obtained himself without great difficulty, if at all, would have given the game away.

There were other problems about the information which were not easily resolved. If a spy's mission was to obtain information about airfields and army installations it would seem reasonable to the army that he should send off the airfield information; disclosures about army installations were, however, a different matter. Needless to say the RAF viewed the situation from a different angle. Clearly, true and verifiable information had to form the greater part of this spy's message if the remainder (the deception) was to be believed. But again great care had to be exercised in the nature of the deceptive message. To say: 'A drunken soldier told me that his unit is practising beach landings and Calais is the expected destination,' would not, of itself, impress a German Intelligence officer. However, a statement such as 'Dover is full of soldiers apparently practising beach landings; it is all very secret but the rumour in the town is that they are planning to land near Calais,' would convince the most hard-headed Abwehr officer if it was linked with an increase in the quantity of intercepted wireless traffic and a report of the sighting of landing craft consigned to the Dover area.

A helpful circumstance during the war was that Hitler believed that the Allies would invade Norway. Any hint of the possibility of this in a series of messages helped to make the entire package credible.

Double Cross — the turning of agents — was, of course, only one aspect of the policy of deception. There were many other people engaged in the task of misleading the Germans and they varied from people who constructed dummy tanks and camouflaged them, to the correspondents who managed to have fictitious items of news hinted at in the neutral press. The camouflage-deception experts invented magnificent deception material which could be packed into a very small area, such as the back of a truck, yet be inflated to deceive aerial reconnaissance. One of the more popular wartime stories was of the dummy airfield complete with wooden planes. It was said that the RAF (or Luftwaffe, in one version) flew over and bombed it with wooden bombs.

Deception tactics provided an outlet for various forms of genius which might otherwise have been wasted. Rommel was lured through soft sand to attack a strong position at Alam

El Halfa by the planting of a deception map (1942). Deception needed a close understanding of German psychology. J.C. Masterman (who chaired the XX Committee) was an Oxford don. Not only did he have a first-class brain, he was also a brilliant all-round games player, notably at hockey, athletics and lawn tennis. However, Masterman's quiet, extremely courteous manner disguised a considerable interest in winning; he was a difficult man to beat. His particular qualification for his XX work was probably acquired during World War I, for he had the misfortune to be in Germany at the outbreak in 1914 and to be interned during the entire four years of the war. There must have been many opportunities for understanding the German military mind which were put to good use later.

Obviously, much deception work was concerned with misleading the enemy over our invasion plans. The first occasion when this was vitally important was in 1942 when we wished to land an army in North Africa in the region of Tunis. It was important not only to deceive the Germans about the particular place chosen for the landing, so that they did not prepare a reception, but it was also important to deceive them into believing that we had other plans. The other plans which we wished them to consider were that the Allies might land in Norway (which they were, as mentioned earlier, ready to expect) or northern France. But it would not be sufficient for the turned spy merely to mention these two possibilities. His (or her) reasons must be convincing, preferably he should have seen some sort of preparations taking place, presumably for Norway or northern France landings. As it happened the Germans were taken completely by surprise by the Torch North African landings but did not blame their spies for not having given them any hint of this possibility. A possible weakness in the deception was the fact that before Torch there was a large build-up of Allied forces around Gibraltar. The Germans doubtless knew this from aerial reconnaissance and therefore the story was put out that the Gibraltar ships were needed for the reinforcement of Malta which was in a parlous state. A possible landing in the Dakar area was also floated as a rumour.

An even more complicated deception was mounted to disguise our plans for a landing in Sicily. The circumstances were somewhat macabre. It was decided that if the body of a staff officer could be washed ashore in Spain, any documents it carried would probably fall into German hands and be very convincing. A suitable body was therefore chosen, dressed in the uniform of an officer of the Royal Marines, kept on ice in a special container and then taken by submarine to a point about a mile off the beach at Huelva. There it was put in the sea and with it a capsized rubber dinghy. The assumption to be made was that the plane carrying the officer had been shot down and that his attempt to escape from the wreckage in his rubber dinghy had failed. As soon as the discovery of the body was notified we began agitating for the return of the papers the officer (fictionally known as Major Martin) was carrying. However, the Spaniards extracted the papers he was carrying without breaking the seals (a practice which had been in use for several hundred years), photographed them and passed the film to the Germans. The vital letter was from Admiral Mountbatten to Admiral Cunningham, the naval commander-in-chief for the Mediterranean theatre. This and another letter indicated that the Allies were not thinking of landing in Sicily at all, but instead in Greece. The result was that the Germans lost much of their interest in Sicily (though not all of it) and instead concentrated forces in Greece and Sardinia. The fictional major was given an official funeral and the tombstone over his grave is still there for the curious to inspect to this day.

In the years which have elapsed since World War II the grimmer aspects of deception have tended to be forgotten and the more amusing aspects publicized. But deception was a game which was played in deadly earnest; if successful it could save many lives whereas if it failed it could be disastrous. The spies with the amusing code names were in a far from happy position. As captured spies they were liable to be shot or hanged and if they did not co-operate that would most probably be their fate. Spies *were* executed in World War II and any captured spy offered the opportunity of being a double-agent knew very well what the alternative was. Over all, spying was a lonely, tedious, nerve-racking activity, very different from the glamorous picture painted by fiction writers. Since World War II the general tolerance of any aberration, coupled with the decline of patriotism in western countries has caused the spy to be regarded more indulgently, although their betrayals were usually for sordid motives and could endanger the lives of millions.

A more wholesome type of information gathering is in what is known as scientific intelligence. This became of immense importance during World War II when it was felt that the enemy might steal a march by inventing some new completely devastating weapon. Hitler was believed to have claimed in 1939 that he had a new and secret weapon which would win the war. From then onward there was constant speculation over what this might be. Conjecture ranged from magnetic mines (which had been known to the British in World War I but neglected) to rockets with atomic warheads. In fact, Hitler was probably referring to the strength of his air force when he was speaking of his secret weapon.

Whether Hitler had a secret weapon or not did not alter the fact that Britain needed an organization both to detect possible enemy inventions and also to encourage and develop our own. The design of the Spitfire and Hurricane fighters had obviously contributed greatly to our winning the Battle of Britain, but an even greater contribution had been made by radar, the system of locating incoming aircraft and ships. Radar had caused the Germans to believe we had more fighters than we actually had. However, early in the war it became obvious that the Germans were using some scientific means of guiding aircraft to their targets. Some indication to this was gained from listening to a conversation between two German prisoners of war. They referred to an X apparatus. This might, of course, be the ordinary navigational aid of a radio beacon or it might be something more complicated. A brilliant young Oxford scientist, R. V. Jones, who was working in the Admiralty Research Establishment, was intrigued by an entry on a scrap of paper salvaged from a shot-down Heinkel bomber. It referred to Radio Beacon Knickebein. Eventually he discovered that Knickebein was a beam along which a bomber could fly to its target and therefore avoid the navigational hazards which can occur when flying over enemy country. It was sadly obvious that whatever system the Germans were using was vastly superior to our own. However, by relentless perseverance and considerable use of intuition Jones worked out what the system must be. One of the devices was code-named 'Wotan' by the Germans and this by a reference to Norse mythology was discovered by Jones originally to be a one-eyed god. One eye, he felt, implied one beam. This turned out to be correct.

The result of these researches was one of the great scientific triumphs of the war. Not only were we able to find out which beams German bombers were travelling along, and thus intercept those beams, but also we were able to affect those beams so that the bombers arrived at a different destination from the one intended. But this was by no means the only contribution to winning the war made by R.V. Jones (later Professor) and his contemporaries.* As each new German weapon came up the scientific committee considered it. To use a wartime expression, they were completely 'unflappable' and their only problem seems to have been occasional internal friction. It is probably inevitable that when a number of exceptionally brilliant and original thinkers are collected together there will be some clash of personalities.

The team could not prevent the launching of the V1 and V2 rockets, but they did much to explain and counter them. One of the counter moves was to bomb the factories where they were manufactured. In the event this was not successful and the menace only ceased when the invasion forces overran the rocket sites themselves. Yet, as R.V. Jones points out, in terms of material damage the V2s did less harm than the bombers. A V2 could deliver a warhead weighing one ton; a bomber could deliver five tons. Rockets which took several months to make and were expendable in fact did much less harm than the bombs delivered by aircraft which mostly returned. But rockets which shot up into the upper atmosphere and came down belching flame were a more potent weapon against morale. The bomber gave warning of its approach; the V2 approached as if by mystery. It would not be entirely true to say that people did not mind being killed by a bomber but took strong exception to being eliminated by the mysterious V2, but there is an element of truth in it.

*See *Most Secret War*: R.V. Jones, Hamish Hamilton, 1978

Communication and intelligence therefore cover an enormous field, most of which we can only touch on. But if there is one area in which wars of today differ most substantially from wars of the past it is undoubtedly this one.

10 The Logistics of Invasion

In all wars one of the most important but least publicized factors has been that of supply or, to use the modern term, logistics. Logistics, in fact, includes the process of moving the troops themselves. To the casual observer it might seem that all an army needs is a good supply of trained fighting men and a leader who knows how to organize them. At the same time the casual observer may have a disquieting memory of the remark attributed to Napoleon that 'an army marches on its stomach', and will therefore consider that food might be a problem on a campaign.

The supply problem, of course, covers a much wider field than food. Even the very earliest invaders, in the dawn of history, had to make sure they had an adequate supply of weapons — perhaps arrows — of food, and of materials for making a shelter for the night. In many lands, and doubtless many seas, lie the bones of those who did not make adequate preparation for the campaigns they set out on. There are some parts of the world where the invader can live off the country, where there will be water even in the hot season, and where the colder weather will not destroy his strength. Invaders who crossed barren desert areas with expectation of finding water often disappeared without trace, and those who ventured into unknown colder regions fared no better.

Some of the problems of the early invaders were of their own making. Some primitive tribes tended to give cattle a social importance which exceeded their value as food. Certain tribes measured their prestige by the number of cattle they produced; a man could not buy a wife unless he possessed a certain number of cattle. Quality was not important but quantity was essential. The word pecuniary derives from the Roman word *pecus* meaning 'head of cattle' and this meaning extended through people far less civilized than the Romans. In primitive societies cattle gave a cause for warfare. As herds grew larger, grazing grounds were exhausted. The tribe moved on, perhaps coming into conflict with other peoples; victory by one side or another diminished the human but not the cattle population. Clearly it would have been wise to have culled the cattle and improved the breed but this would have offended the ethos of the tribe. Caught up in a culture in which cattle were synonymous with food, wealth and prestige, the tribe would invade new territory, sustained by meat 'on the hoof' but dependent on victory for new grazing lands by which alone the cattle (and tribe) would be able to survive.

By no means all primitive people were caught in this vicious circle of needing new lands to survive and soon afterwards having to move on lest their present supplies should be diminished; there were also people who depended on hunting and moved on to more prolific hunting grounds and there were early farmers who moved because unwittingly they had exhausted the lands they existed on. But even in such primitive communities moves could not be made without planning and preparation. Reserves of weapons would be needed, for arrows would be expended and spears broken. Tools, cooking materials, perhaps even clothing, would need to be carried. Early life may have been primitive but it was not as lacking in organization as is widely believed.

Unfortunately there is little on record about the logistical arrangements of the early invaders. It is obvious that campaigners like Alexander the Great and Julius Caesar must have had considerable supply trains, and their protection must have given much concern. The longer the supply train, the greater its vulnerability; an attack on an unguarded flank could easily separate the head from the tail with disastrous results for both. It seems likely that Roman armies in the later stages of the Empire had too many supplies, not least of which would be wine.

The Normans who invaded England in 1066 and won the Battle of Hastings had a well-developed logistical system.

They brought over horses, which are notoriously bad sailors, adequate supplies of armour and weapons, and pre-fabricated castles to be used against any counter-attack. It seems probable that just as Harold did not know of William's impending arrival — which was dependent on a change in the wind — William was equally unaware that when he arrived the English king would have been drawn away to the north. Most probably William expected to be attacked soon after landing, the fact that he was unmolested and did not encounter the English army until he had pushed nearly seven miles inland must have struck him as an unexpected piece of good luck.

William had brought in the age of feudalism, which for practical purposes meant the age of the horse, the armourer, the smith, the administrator, the legislator, the mason and the priest. 'He covered the land with castles', a contemporary reported; furthermore he sent clerks to every quarter to list every material object in this newly conquered land. The result was the 'Domesday Book' from which William and his successors could calculate exactly how much each land-holding could contribute to the sinews of war. Once established, this catalogue of the potential wealth of the country was the basis for the logistical support of every subsequent campaign. When Richard I set off on the Third Crusade in 1189 his baggage train included armour, arrows, and even fifty thousand horseshoes. Later in the Crusade we find him transporting specially hard stone from Sicily to be used in catapults against the citadel of Acre. Other wars of this period had similar logistical problems, which they solved ruthlessly. Churches were demolished to make siege engines, and so on.

In general, armies could never live successfully off the countries they invaded. Once the captured towns had been plundered there was little to do but to move on or to retreat. To stay might be to risk starvation in a besieged town or devastated countryside. Large armies were never a practical proposition in the Middle Ages. A large army might win a battle but God was certainly never on the side of the big battalions when it came to feeding them. Centuries later Wellington said of Spain that it was a country where small armies got beaten and large armies starved. The same could have been said of

France, Germany, Russia and Italy during the Middle Ages. If an army was to survive it was important for it to move quickly through the countryside, as the Mongols did. Most of the campaigns undertaken by medieval armies in western Europe petered out through a combination of disease, lack of supplies, and general inertia. Continuous rain, swollen rivers, impassable tracks and ruined food supplies, are mentioned with great regularity in accounts of medieval campaigns. The English Channel undoubtedly was a great impediment to any French invasion of Britain but equally it was a considerable advantage to France for English kings, such as Edward III and Henry V, were limited in their ambitions by the amount of men and materials they could transport across the water.

As we come nearer to our own times it is clear that the logistical problem increased faster than any other. The age of gunpowder brought in the problem of transporting heavier materials; siege guns were a particular problem. Later, in the eighteenth century, the problem of obtaining and transporting forage for horses could influence the tactics, or even the feasibility of a campaign.

In the Napoleonic Wars, as is well known, the French expedition to Moscow ended in disaster because the logistical problem had been completely underestimated. Originally Napoleon had ordered fifty days' supply of bread and rice for 400,000 men, and oats for 50,000 horses for the same period. Huge dumps of food were established in Poland. The supplies were to be transported by a waggon train consisting of seventeen battalions, a vast force but totally inadequate for the purpose. Most of the vehicles (6,000 in total) failed to reach their destination owing to bad roads and lack of discipline. Horses were soon being fed off the thatch from cottages, and green rye. Soon, cold, rain and starvation had killed off 8,000 of the horses but many of the men were too weak and dispirited to be able to collect firewood and cook the flesh. And this was only the outward journey. The Russians had left nothing they could carry away or destroy; in this they were like the Gallic leader Vercingetorix retreating in front of Julius Caesar nearly two thousand years earlier, and as the Russians would be again over a hundred years later. The story of the French retreat from Moscow through the Russian winter is too well known to need repeating here.

But long before the Moscow campaign the drain of French resources was beginning to affect Napoleon's campaigning ability. It is not perhaps widely appreciated that the stranglehold on supplies which was caused by Napoleon's own Berlin Decrees and later reinforced by the Orders in Council did more to weaken the French armies than their mounting total of casualties.

The importance of supplies to an army in the field was probably not fully realized by the general public until the Crimean campaign. In 1854 Britain and France and Russia began a war of attrition on the Crimea Peninsula. Britain and France were some hundreds of miles from their bases; the Russians had an extremely difficult overland route and the British a combination of land and sea. The assumption that the war would rapidly be concluded with a few swift glamorous battles was soon proved to be unfounded. As the armies settled down to the harsh winter on the bleak Crimea Peninsula, the lack of forethought and preparation for the campaign was all too apparent. Much-needed supplies were sent but were not unloaded quickly enough and were wrecked in Balaclava harbour. Men and horses died of starvation and disease. Frantic efforts to alleviate the situation produced some results but also such bizarre occurrences as the despatch of five thousand left-foot boots and a supply of children's clothing which would not fit even the smallest soldier. The scandal of it all was publicized by newspaper correspondents (which gave some comfort to enemy intelligence) but also roused such public indignation that the situation was rectified. The war dragged on for another year but by that time supplies of every essential commodity were pouring into the Crimea.

However, new and unexpected problems were now developing. One of these was over food. Armies fighting in tropical countries needed special supplies which varied from clothing to food. The introduction of Indian troops into British-directed campaigns caused unexpected headaches to quartermasters. Hindus regarded cattle as sacred while Moslems regarded the pig as unclean. Special cooking arrangements were essential; religion now affected logistics.

In the nineteenth century it seemed as if the railway was the answer to most of the quartermaster's problems. Troops, ammunition, guns and supplies could now be transported at speed to the places where they were most needed. A spy observing the traffic along a railway track would be thought to be earning his money well. And, before the day of the bomber and of long-range artillery, it was difficult to interfere with a railway system.

One of the most successful uses of a railway was made by Kitchener in his invasion of the Sudan in 1898. In 1883 the British had been bundled unceremoniously out of the Sudan by the followers of the Mahdi, the Dervishes, and General Gordon had been killed in the process. The task of recovering the country and delivering it from the tyranny of fanaticism was given to Kitchener, who would later lay the foundation of success in World War I by his recruiting plans. Kitchener, who was an engineer, considered that the reconquest of the Sudan, which is inhospitable country covering a million square miles, could only be made by an efficiently supplied army. Building a railway was an essential part of his plan and by 1898 his army, supplied by the railway and supported by gunboats on the Nile, was able to defeat a huge army of Dervishes at Omdurman.

The railway was again employed by Kitchener as a military instrument in the South African War of 1899–1902 (the Boer War). In the opening stages the British fared badly against the mobile, lightly equipped Boer farmers who knew the country and used cover and terrain to best advantage. When appointed to command, Kitchener quickly realized that the key to defeating the Boers was to cut off their supplies; even the most adventurous guerrilla cannot continue to fight if he is deprived of supplies. Kitchener's tactics were to use the railways to supply the British force while at the same time clearing one area after another of potential supplies for the Boers. His method was known as the blockhouse system, for he wired each cleared sector and protected it against reoccupation by strong-points. The inhabitants of those areas, who had been supplying the Boer guerrillas, were moved to camps for the duration of the war. The policy of concentrating the Boers in camps undoubtedly shortened the war, but the fact that the term 'concentration camps' was used by the Nazis for their

mass-extermination camps in 1939–45 gave the words a reputation which the South African camps certainly did not
deserve. It is, however, true that the death rate from disease in
those camps was appallingly high, as it was among all those
engaged in the campaign. Typhus, enteric fever, and dysen-
tery were some of the killers. The British have been blamed for
the death rate in the Boer camps but a good proportion of it
was caused by the Boers' failure to exercise normal sanitary
precautions. Subsequently, in World War II when the Japanese
held large numbers of British and Dutch prisoners of war, and
gave them endless work, little food, and no medicines, the
death rate among the Dutch was much higher than among the
British. Too many of the Dutch were indifferent to the
requirements of camp hygiene until the lesson had been learnt
in the bitterest possible way.

In World War I Kitchener was again engaged in the logistical side and seems to have been the only member of the Higher
Command who sensed that the war might be a long one. In
consequence he made provision for recruiting armies of vastly
greater size than anyone else had thought either necessary or
possible. Appropriately he has been termed 'the architect of
victory'. However, Kitchener was dead before the war with its
vast supply problems was fully into its stride. It was said that it
took eight men to keep one man in the front line but if all the
people engaged on the production of food, clothing and munitions were counted, this would probably be an underesti-
mate. Dividing the number of rounds fired by the number of
men killed gives us 50,000 rounds to kill one man. Stupendous
quantities of materials — and men — were assembled, transported across the Channel, conveyed to the front line and then
expended in the most wasteful way imaginable. The Germans
could not afford to be any less prodigal. In their opening move
of the war, the Schlieffen Plan, two of their armies had outdis-
tanced their supplies and also lost direction. The plan for
lightning victory settled into a four years' war of attrition.

A great problem of modern large-scale war is the space and
time required for the movement of troops and their supplies.
In the nineteenth century it was estimated that when two
divisions— a mere fragment of a modern army— were moved
along a road thirty feet wide they would extend over $21\frac{1}{2}$ miles.

The column would include 500 vehicles and a number of horses. A World War I column of this size would march for two or three days, covering, if lucky, some twenty miles a day. On occasions the route of one column would cross that of another. The confusion and chaos may be imagined.

Whether troops march, or are conveyed, there are enormous problems. Start a column of 300 men in three files marching over a reasonably uncluttered route. Within three miles the men at the front will be virtually marking time, while those at the back will be running to keep up. Put them in vehicles and start them at five-minute intervals. Every time there is a crossroads those behind will lose more ground until they have almost lost touch.

If the supply situation is a problem in static warfare such as World War I, it rapidly becomes a nightmare in mobile warfare as in World War II. The very instruments of mobility, the trucks, tanks, aircraft and self-propelled guns, are themselves creators of supply problems, for they all require petrol, oil and lubricants (POL, as the army terms them). The fact that firepower has increased means that more guns can fire bigger shells more rapidly. Tanks, which are considerably more complicated than they look from the outside, are made up of several thousand components and many of those components are likely to go wrong and need repair or replacing. A 'knocked-out' tank needs to be recovered from a forward area, or the enemy may recover it and use it against you. Captured materials must be transported backwards while your own requirements are coming forward. Casualties, whether human or material, are sent to the rear, thus helping to block the routes which are badly needed for up-traffic. When the Germans invaded Russia in 1941 they had a good supply of Russian maps and therefore knew the Russian road system. Unfortunately for the Germans many of the roads marked on the maps had never been made; the maps had been printed according to someone's optimistic forecast. The importance of the few roads which existed was soon made clear to the Germans, for in the wet weather heavy vehicles which strayed off them were liable to be bogged down for ever.

Information soon came back that more powerful guns were needed to deal with T34 tanks. The Germans had several types of gun — 20-mm, 37-mm, 50-mm, 75-mm and 88-mm, among others. Apart from difference in calibre there were other specifications such as whether the shell was for anti-personnel use, armour-piercing, or anti-aircraft. Not least of the German troubles was the fact that the wrong ammunition was frequently delivered and had to be re-routed, thus blocking urgently needed supply lines. All these problems occurred without any assistance from enemy bombing or shelling. The Germans launched 145 divisions into Russia in 1941, estimating that this would be ample and that the campaign would be over in ten weeks. As the Germans pushed deeper into Russia their supply problems grew. Rain, mud, snow, cold, heat, dust, all seemed to be ranged against them. Ominously, Barbarossa had begun on the anniversary of Napoleon's invasion of Russia.

In other theatres of World War II the supply problem was no less pressing and vulnerable. In the western desert almost all food was smothered in flies as a man tried to eat, and all vehicles suffered in varying degrees from the effects of sand. Proving tests of vehicles in temperate zones were found to have little relevance to desert conditions. There were other problems as the war dragged on. Troops will endure boredom, spartan rations and lack of entertainment without much complaint when the duration of a campaign is short and when the objective can be seen clearly. In long-drawn-out campaigns however 'comforts for the troops' become more important and 'essential supplies' have to include books, letters, entertainers, music, and fleshly comforts such as alcohol, chocolate and plentiful cigarettes. When the Americans took the field it was felt by the more austerely served British soldiers that the scale of United States 'creature comforts' erred well on the side of luxury. However the American government's ability to provide was not limited to the comforts of its servicemen; it also covered a range of lethal equipment, ranging from Sherman tanks to B29 bombers, and jeeps to six-ton trucks, which were a decisive factor in the Allied war effort.

The multiplicity of articles needed to keep an army in the field gave fresh opportunities to a new type of soldier, and to some extent to resistance workers. This was the expert in behind-the-lines work and sabotage. In the western desert when it was obvious that the German bombers were faster than our fighters and we therefore could not easily cope with them in the air, an enterprising young lieutenant named David Stirling managed to create a small private army which ventured deep into the desert, crept on to German airfields at night and blew up parked planes. The Germans were caught in a dilemma of wondering whether to spare troops to guard installations several hundred miles behind their front line or whether to hope for the best. They compromised and Stirling was therefore able to destroy 350 aircraft and numerous other military objects; this was the beginning of the Special Air Service (SAS). A similar policy was implemented in France where the main targets were railway lines, brigades, trains, and ammunition dumps. Under normal conditions such activities have a considerable nuisance value: in time of crisis they may exercise great influence on the outcome of a campaign. Just before D-Day in June 1944, SAS units and partisans blew up considerable stretches of railway track and several bridges. The delay this caused to reinforcements and materials destined for the fighting areas was well beyond expectations. In one part of the operation the Paris–Chalon-sur-Saône railway line was cut over twenty times. When an invasion occurs the defending country has the choice between whether to repel it on the beachhead, but then face the fact that it might be able to be successful in a different area, or let it land with good proportions of its supplies, then counter-attack and destroy it. In the event the Germans were prevented from giving full effect to any ideas they may have had about destroying the Allies at the beachhead because they were deceived about the landing point; later they were prevented from bringing their full force to bear on the counter-attack by the interruptions to their supply routes.

Many interesting discoveries were made about armoured fighting vehicles in World War II. One was that a single tank immobilized on a road could delay a whole armoured regiment until it was moved. Secondly, the destructive power of a tank could ultimately impede both itself and others if used unwisely. Thus a tank which entered a village shelling the houses in a manner which caused them to collapse across the route could make that road a very poor means of communication for other vehicles, including tanks. Thirdly, a tank could reach the end of its tether through running out of fuel, ammunition, or spares. After the Panzers had so successfully torn apart the Allied armies in France in 1940 Hitler gave the order to halt outside Dunkirk. The order was not, as has been naively supposed, based on a wish not to destroy the army of the British Empire, but on the assumption that the tanks had now covered so much ground that they could not be in a fit state for further action. To commit them further would be to risk their loss in a determined counter-attack by desperate men, it was thought. In view of the condition of many of the troops beleaguered in Dunkirk, the possibility of an effective counter-attack seems improbable but the assessment ·that, after covering over forty miles a day for several days, the tanks would have exhausted themselves and outrun their supplies is a reasonable one.

Because of the proximity of the D-Day landing beaches most Europeans seem unaware that on the other side of the world another series of highly organized landings took place in the same period. The Japanese had entered the war in 1941 without benefit of declaration and had crippled the American navy at Pearl Harbor. They had gone on to capture the Philippines, Malaya, Burma, Java, Sumatra and a number of Pacific islands. They had given little attention to supplying their invasion armies, calculating that as Orientals they could live off the country. Owing to Western ineptitude, the initial Japanese moves were very successful. They captured huge quantities of supplies which included oil from Borneo, and rubber from Malaya, both vital strategic materials. They almost reached Australia but there, as also on the frontiers of India, they were checked. Then began the slow march home. American land and naval forces, under determined commanders such as MacArthur and Nimitz, captured one Japanese stronghold after another. The Japanese fought with astonishing courage and tenacity to hold the beaches but were eventually swept away not merely by the sheer weight of metal but by unlimited American courage too. But the key to it was logistics. After a devastating initial bombardment American landing craft discharged their human contents on to the beaches where they were supplied and reinforced. American bulldozers moved in the jungle, cleared it, flattened it, and had aircraft landing and taking off within hours. Japanese communications were cut by submarine and aerial warfare and as the US bases came closer, Japanese factories on the main islands came under a daily pounding from American bombers. It is now reported that many Japanese knew that their country had lost the war when the Pearl Harbor attack failed to cripple all the American Pacific Fleet, some of it being at sea at the time. If so, they kept quiet about it although they were right. Likewise, Albert Speer, Minister of Production in Nazi Germany, is reported to have said in 1943 that Germany would lose the war because it could never match the American supply system, but it seems unlikely that he addressed his remarks to Hitler.

Since 1945 there have been further experiences in logistics which have afforded lessons. In Korea the problem was one of too much transport for the road system, and a reluctance to leave the roads and take to the countryside in normal infantry work. The multiplication of mobility has caused congestion in other theatres, of which the most obvious was Vietnam. Vietnam however was not lost because the Americans had too much transport: it was lost because they hesitated to wage the only sort of war which would have produced a victory. It would have involved bombing the main North Vietnam ports and supply routes and doubtless damaging the ships of so-called neutral countries in the process. So America fought the war half-heartedly, unconvinced even of the rightness of her cause. Now that it is too late, and tyrannies have established themselves in the lands which America no longer tries to protect, the critics of American policy have fallen silent.

From the purely military point of view the great contribution to logistical development made by the Vietnam war was the development of the helicopter. Helicopters were once thought to be too vulnerable to be used in forward areas but armed helicopters can give a very good account of themselves. And for the evacuation of casualties or for bringing up supplies to beleaguered outposts they are unmatchable.

'History repeats itself because geography remains a constant.' Early armies had to make detours to avoid deep rivers, tangled forests, even marshy ground. A mere brook can become an almost impassable obstacle when several hundred men have forded it, and some perhaps have left their bodies in it. When vehicles were used they depended on roads and bridges and as more and more men and horses were included in armies the longer the supply trains grew. Guns, ammunition, materials to make or break the fortifications, fuel, food, replacements, all added to the bulk behind the fighting men. In recent years provision for welfare has added to the burden. The art of war now incorporates the science of logistics and the techniques of mass production. But not entirely. Ultimately the infantryman must stand on the conquered though devastated ground.

11 Resistance

Some invaders have no illusion about the hatred which their arrival arouses. They will expect active or passive resistance and be prepared. Others may feel they are being welcomed as liberators. They will eye the cheering crowds as they pass by but if they are wise they will reflect that among those welcomers there are perhaps some who harbour very different thoughts.

Resistance will reveal itself at different stages and in diverse ways. It may take the form of sabotage at the docks where goods are unloaded, and may lead to the derailment of trains, it may lead to a series of inexplicable accidents, or it may show itself in a sullen lack of co-operation with the newcomers.

Resistance may be a planned military operation or it may result from the adventurous nature of a few restless young men and women. It may centre around a single figure, as Che Guevara, or Joan of Arc. It may be the result of professed political or religious conviction. Whatever the causes it can be very dangerous to the invader and ultimately show him in the worst possible light.

'Resistance', which was a creditable wartime activity against invaders who occupied the resisters' homelands, has now become a terrorist activity for dubious political motives. Some terrorism seems to have no point or purpose in it but to be the result of unbalanced minds. Unfortunately this corrupt version of what was once a brave and skilful method of fighting has tended to diminish the respect in which wartime agents were held and which was undoubtedly their due.

All forms of resistance require great courage and enormous

self-discipline. The first category of resistance fighter we shall discuss is the stay-behind operator. This is a man or woman who has been prepared for sabotage behind the enemy line and probably been supplied with basic requirements and training for it. It comes as a surprise to many people to learn that there were stay-behind parties organized for Kent and Sussex in the event of a German invasion in 1940. This was in addition to the units of the Home Guard, originally called the Local Defence Volunteers, which had enrolled all able-bodied men between seventeen and sixty-five. (One member of the Home Guard managed to enlist and serve undetected at the age of eighty, but he was a former soldier.)

The stay-behind parties were officially designated 'Auxiliary Units' and the intention was that they should consist of one or two army officers and some suitable members of the Home Guard. Twenty such units were organized and furnished with bases and equipment. Each auxiliary unit had links to small sections of the Home Guard; as the members of the latter were normally resident in the areas concerned it was felt that their local knowledge would be useful. No unit had more than sixteen members and the commander was usually a second-lieutenant. Their bases were somewhat crude and uncomfortable. Although they were underground they relied less on that fact for safety than that they were in woodland or scrub. The weakness of their position was that they were necessarily static and that in the course of a few weeks the tracks leading to and from the hide-outs would be visible from the air and most probably from the ground too. Aerial photography can pick out a track which is scarcely visible from the ground. A man crossing a field with dew on it— which is what would undoubtedly happen — leaves a track clearly visible from the air. Several converging tracks . . . and that is the end of an auxiliary unit. Camouflage of the hide-out from aerial observation is not particularly difficult if you have materials such as scrim nets and a good understanding of the principle of concealment, but the sort of camouflage which makes a hide-out invisible from the air would be hardly missed by a foot-patrol. Attempts to communicate by wireless from one unit to another would not have been undetected by radio monitors, and the use of messengers would have been hazardous.

All this suggests that a technique of warfare which worked very well in large countries such as France, Italy or Burma, or could work in small countries such as Malaya where there was thick jungle for concealment, faced a number of hazards in England. The chances are that the rural guerrilla would not have lasted very long but have been quite effective in his lifetime; on the other hand the urban guerrilla would have had a good run for his money but been less effective militarily owing to such handicaps as the curfew. The problem with all guerrilla units is that if they keep a low profile they are of little or no value but if they engage in activities which make the enemy take notice and action over their presence they cause brutal reprisals to fall on to innocent people.

However, before dismissing the Auxiliary Units as naive and probably useless concepts it is important to consider the mental climate of the time. The British Expeditionary Force had been bundled out of France but rescued for the most part by little boats. In fact the navy did most of the rescuing but the story that it had been done by little men in little boats manned by volunteers was good for national morale. Besides, had not Churchill said:

> Even though large tracts of Europe and many old and famous states have fallen, or may fall, into the grip of the Gestapo and all the odious apparatus of Nazi rule, we shall not flag or fail. We shall go on to the end, we shall fight in France, we shall fight on the seas and oceans, we shall fight with growing confidence and growing strength in the air, we shall defend our island whatever the cost may be, we shall fight on the beaches, we shall fight on the landing grounds, we shall fight in the fields and in the streets, we shall fight in the hills; we shall never surrender . . .

Here was something the rest of the nation could and would do. Woe betide the handsome young German soldier who picked up a British girl and walked towards a dark lane; he would be unlikely to return. Woe betide the German invader who thought he could now relax a little and get to know some of the local farmers. Such soldiers might in themselves be innocent and well-meaning but they were the instruments by which Gestapo torture and SS concentration camps could appear in this country. No one would have any compassion for them; they must be killed. The Auxiliary Units might not be the final answer, or even one of them, but they pointed the way.

As the main German invasion was expected to come through Kent and Sussex it is not surprising that the forward headquarters of the Auxiliary Units was at a farmhouse called The Garth at Bilting, just off the Canterbury–Maidstone road. The Garth was not only a headquarters but also a training centre where every Sunday members of the Auxiliary Units were trained in various orthodox and unorthodox ways of killing. It was officially known as XII Corps Observation Unit and there were twenty others like it in various parts of the British Isles. The Garth had the good fortune to be commanded by Peter Fleming, author and explorer, brother of Ian Fleming, the creator of James Bond. In spite of its official backing the Garth was a most unofficial establishment for no paper records were kept of the personnel involved. The Gestapo would have had even less compunction than usual at shooting the members out of hand if they had ever caught up with them.

Apart from The Garth there were other training centres. One was at Coleshill in Buckinghamshire, and another at Osterley Park. A leading figure in the art of guerrilla warfare was Tom Wintringham who had been a soldier in World War I and subsequently commanded the British battalion in the International Brigade in Spain. Wintringham wrote a 'Penguin Special' called *New Ways of War*. It was published in 1940 and drew on his experiences between 1936 and 1939 when fighting with the ill-equipped International Brigade against the vastly better equipped German and Italian 'volunteers' in Spain. It was essentially practical. Wintringham thought little of anti-tank mines or petrol bombs. He noted that there were plenty of hand grenades in the country and felt that these should be used as much as possible. He could see no value in the 12-bore shot gun unless the cartridge was suitably doctored. He suggested that the pellets should be taken out of the container, melted down and reinserted in the cartridge to make one large slug. And 'there is one great principle for any road block. It is useless unless covered with weapons.' He goes on to describe the best types of road block but also assesses the possibilities of the ones that might have to be used in an emergency.

Writing a little later, but considerably before 1942 when the booklet was published, Alfred Kerr produced an admirable guide entitled *Guerrilla*. The publishers wrote on the front cover: 'Every Home Guard and serving soldier *must* read this book', and the author clearly believed that if we invaded the continent of Europe with infiltrated guerrillas instead of planning a large military operation the war would quickly be over.

These, of course, were surrounded by a mass of other pamphlets advising people on everything from keeping chickens and pigs on scraps to creating tank obstacles. There was great apprehension about parachutists, and both regular army units and volunteers 'stood to' at dawn and dusk and watched the skies for airborne invaders. Numerous rumours passed eagerly from one area to another. Some of the warning messages reached heights of nonsense which now seem scarcely credible. Poisoned chocolates were said to have been dropped — fifty miles away. Parachutists dressed up as nuns and concealed hand-grenades in their voluminous garments. Everyone was urged to be on guard against the machinations of the Fifth Columnist. The term came from Spain where Franco, approaching a town with four columns, said he had a fifth working for him in the city. Even if one could do nothing else to frustrate a possible German invasion attempt one could at least do one's bit in keeping a watchful eye for Fifth Columnists. Bogus nuns and priests were said to have preceded the Germans in Belgium and prevented bridges being blown up. It was no fun being a nun or priest in Britain in 1940; everyone looked at you most suspiciously. Strangers were automatically the object of suspicion. But, of course, there were strangers everywhere. Some had been evacuated from London, like the BBC and employees of large firms, others were people who normally lived in areas which were now official military danger zones.

On the Continent resistance had reached a more sophisticated and dangerous stage. The enemy was already there. You did not have to watch out for his arrival; it was all too easy to see him and his vehicles, to read his notices and unwillingly learn his rules. If your village was occupied and you felt you might be dragooned into a labour force you probably deserted your home and your possessions and tried to find somewhere the Germans had not yet occupied. There were various ways you could try to restore your self-respect, so diminished by defeat. You could spread anti-German stories, you could look at them with hatred and contempt, you could steal from them. Even to be a black marketeer was an outlet for some.

You could keep your eyes and ears open about what the Germans were doing. Some day the information might be useful to someone. You would begin to feel you were resisting. You noted not merely the presence of a tank but its size, armament and approximate speed. You had begun to collect military data. You kept quiet about what you had noted: walls have ears. If you were the sort of person who is accustomed to mind his own business, you must stop being that sort of person and instead develop an insatiable curiosity. If a German asked you a question you knew nothing, had seen nothing. Meanwhile you accumulated a store of information which might one day be useful.

It is difficult in times of peace to realize what can be of vital interest in wartime. The weather suddenly becomes immensely important. There were no weather forecasts or reports broadcast or in the press in World War II; they could be of great value to the enemy airforce or invasion fleet. However, even inside a country knowledge of the weather pattern could be an asset. Most people have a reasonably sound idea of the weather in their own district; equally they are usually completely ignorant of the weather pattern in other areas. There is much folklore about weather which is not true. Winter does not end in March, to be followed by spring and summer. In some people's minds there is a conviction that there is a normal pattern to the British weather. The reality is different. A few years ago in Britain there was snow in the beginning of June and drought at the end of it. The bloodiest battle on English soil was at Towton on 29th March 1461. It was fought in a snowstorm. And if the tricks of the weather are disconcerting enough in Europe or Russia they are ten times more so in the tropics and sub-tropics. Who would expect frost or flood in the desert? Who would go to war in the south-west monsoon?

All this information which could be collected by anyone came under the heading of general intelligence. Even more important was specific economic intelligence. Few people know or care what is being made in factories in their district but an alert mind might discover, in wartime, that a rare type of gun, a new cipher machine, a new rocket, or a new form of chemical agent was being manufactured. Ball-bearings may not seem of great military importance; anyone can make them. However the fact that nearly all German ball-bearing manufacture was concentrated in one area caused the RAF to give that area its special attention. Oil is an obvious strategic material but equally valuable is the route it takes. You and you alone may know where an aeroplane crashed. It might have come down at night, in the depths of a wood, or in a marsh. Someone better qualified than you perhaps would wish to take a closer look, so you pass the information to the right quarter. Even odd sheets of paper blowing around in the street might be useful; they could have fallen out of a staff officer's brief-case.

Helping people to escape was very dangerous work. Escapers could be spies, prisoners of war, or more probably crashed air crew. The latter formed the bulk of the traffic along the escape lines, all through France and Spain. It was immensely important work, for pilots and air crew took much longer to train than aircraft took to build. You might hide an escaper yourself or you might organize a network in your district.

Sabotage could be another activity. For preference it should not be obvious. Making dud shells was one form of it but the Germans were not fools and they kept an eye open for such sabotage. Putting in the wrong type of oil was another ploy, or even quietly pouring away some vital lubricant. Railway workers could be very useful if they changed round the labels on goods. Anti-aircraft batteries who had indented for spares would not perhaps be overjoyed at receiving a consignment of agricultural machinery (badly needed elsewhere); they would tend to blame their own government rather than suspect sabotage.

But what no one should forget is that any, even the most

minor form of resistance, was carried on in an atmosphere of fear and uncertainty. Perhaps a member of the occupying force might feel you were taking a little too much interest in him, his rank or his work. The secret police could call on you at three a.m. perhaps, and take you away, before you had time to dress, to await questioning in a police cell. At the same time your family could be taken away — to somewhere else. You might never see them again. To be awaiting questioning by the Gestapo or Japanese Kempei was not an experience to relish. Perhaps you had been denounced by a collaborator. There were such people in every country. War brings out the best in people but also the worst.

In World War II certain countries were so long under German occupation that it became a way of life. France was defeated in 1940 and for four years it must have seemed to many French people that, as had happened after the 1870 war, the Germans would remain until they chose to leave. A number of people came to terms with the fact of being a country under German rule; having experienced the German war machine it was difficult to imagine its being beaten.

However, in the occupied countries of Europe there were sparks to keep the flame alive. Some Frenchmen were taken away — you may see memorials to them in certain parts of France — because they were suspected of subversive activities, and they were never seen again. There was a deep and unrelenting hatred of the German conqueror which was stimulated when he made efforts to be friendly.

Men were perhaps more likely to forget a national humiliation than women were. Many men make a deliberate effort to forget. Women are less prone to deceiving themselves in such matters. Women therefore tended to make much better agents, being sustained by deep memories. They were also likely to be cooler in emergencies and more plausible. Often their courage exceeded that of men but some met appalling fates, such as being burnt alive in a furnace by the Gestapo.

Resistance groups in World War II varied enormously in quality. Some were active; some lazy. Some were keener to embarrass rival groups than they were to damage the occupying power. Force 136 in Malaya incorporated a number of enthusiastic Communists includings the notorious Chin Peng.

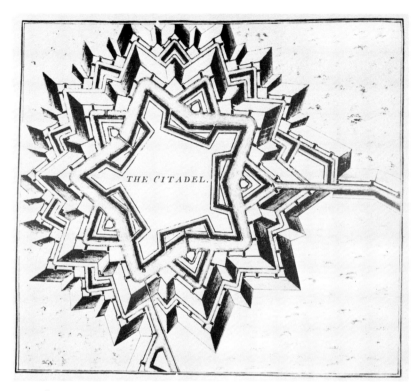

A star fort

'The real View of the FRENCH RAFT as intended for the Invasion of ENGLAND.
Drawn from the Original at Brest.' The raft is powered by windmills

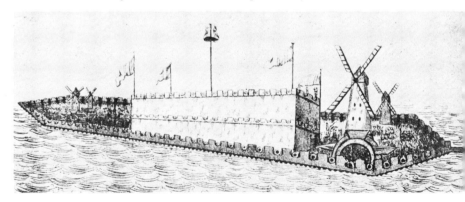

'John Bull Arming' — a cartoon from the Napoleonic Wars, c. 1798

A fireship. Note that the ports hinge downwards so that they do not close while she burns

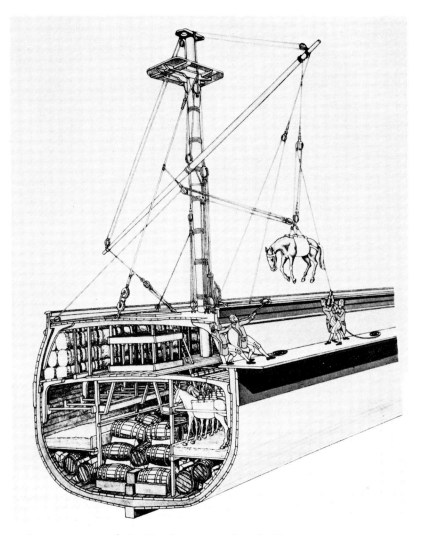

A horse transport of the Napoleonic period, a highly
specialised vessel

The Martello tower at Dymchurch

Part of Fort Widley, one of the Portsdown forts, showing an entrance to the underground tunnels

HMS *Bellerophon* in 1907, one of the Dreadnoughts

Two octagonal pillboxes, one disguised as a haystack and the other disguised with disruptive camouflage

Flame on the beaches — part of the anti-invasion defences

Opposite an uncamouflaged pillbox, showing gun slits

Flame-thrower defences at Newhaven Harbour

A YMCA tea car at an airfield gun pit. The aircraft is a
Hampden bomber

August 1940. Night-fighter pilots waiting in the Orders
Room of a Fighter Command Station

A group called the People's Malayan Anti-Japanese Army changed its name immediately after Japan was defeated and became the People's Anti-British Army. 'Resistance' armies had often hidden away guns and equipment which had been sent for use against Germans or Japanese; later they were brought into use in the struggle for 'independence', which meant the establishment of a left-wing government. To those supplies were added many given by the Japanese or Germans who, instead of surrendering their arms to the Allies, gave them to the forces most likely to cause trouble in the future.

Although they did much good work, resistance organizations were a peculiar and varied collection. Most of them were highly individualistic and would take orders from no one. Many included numbers of people who would never settle down easily to a peaceful existence. But whatever their gains in terms of successes against the enemy they all had the virtue of preserving national identity. The fact that France had a number of active resistance groups kept in being a feeling of national pride in spite of the humiliation inflicted by the deceits, treacheries and failures which had led to the crushing and unnecessary defeat of 1940.

If Britain had fallen and Germany had won the war, it seems likely that the Gestapo and SS would have made a special effort to stamp out any spark of resistance. Massacres such as that at Oradour and Lidice would probably have been commonplace. It would have been a time of horror and fear. But eventually the slaughter and the torture would have to come to an end. At that point a new resistance would have been born and it would have been fully as ruthless as the force it was opposing. It might have taken years to achieve any real success, but one day without doubt its chance would have come.

12 Operation 'Sealion'

By July 1940 Germany had completed an impressive total of conquests. To her acquisitions of the pre-war years, which included Austria and Czechoslovakia, she had now added most of Poland and all of Norway, Denmark, Belgium, Holland and France. The fact that southern France was ruled nominally by the Vichy government did not mean that it was any the less under German control. There was only one obstacle to the completion of Hitler's plans to overrun western Europe before turning to attack Russia. That was Britain and, as the British army had been lucky to escape from Dunkirk, although leaving all its equipment behind, it did not seem as though the last obstacle to German hegemony should be a very serious one. In fact the position of Britain after France had fallen seemed so precarious that Hitler fully expected that surrender terms would immediately be agreed. He was said to be an admirer of Britain and the British Empire and unwilling to extinguish the British spirit completely.

It soon became clear to Hitler, as was already suspected by his service chiefs, that this mildly benevolent attitude was not going to be reciprocated. The Luftwaffe had been given orders not to bomb Britain during July so that Churchill would not be stimulated into unnecessary resistance. This scenario was somewhat upset by the pugnacity of Churchill's speeches and the growing conviction that Britain would fight to the end, however bitter. On 25th July the ban on bombing Britain was lifted and full consideration given to invasion plans, first called 'Lion' and later *Seeloewe* (Sealion).

However it was one thing to decide that Sealion was feasible but another to implement it. There had been an earlier plan, produced in November 1939, in which the German General Staff had explored the possibility of landing in East Anglia. Curiously enough, the East Anglian plan followed the lines of a story by Frank H. Shaw, 'The Swoop of the Eagle', which had been published in the boys' magazine *Chums* in 1913. Each instalment had been prefaced with the remark: 'Notice— This story is not intended to stir up race hatred but is written as a true picture of what would happen if a great continental nation attacked our country — Your Editor.' Fortunately the story ended with the capture of the Kaiser, who had unwisely landed to see how things were going. Frank H. Shaw wrote another invasion story in *Chums* in the 1920s; this time the invasion was by a combined force of Russians and Chinese!

But in July 1940 there was nothing fictional about the danger facing Britain. Goering claimed that he could sweep the Royal Air Force out of the skies. The German General Staff was used to Goering's boasts and accepted this one with reservations. The higher ranks of the Luftwaffe were well aware of the fight that the RAF had put up in France, at the cost of close on a thousand aeroplanes. This left less than five hundred for the defence of Britain although, fortunately for us, the Luftwaffe did not realize how few there were. Even at best Fighter Command never made up to more than three-quarters of the numbers which had been lost in France.

However, if the Luftwaffe had doubts, the German naval staff had even more serious reservations. At sea the Germans were hopelessly outclassed, having suffered severe losses in the Norway campaign. The British Home Fleet alone had five battleships and eleven cruisers. If the Luftwaffe had been able to establish complete air superiority over the Channel the disparity in naval strength might not have mattered. But the Luftwaffe could not.

Another shortcoming was in landing craft. Most of the 2,000 barges and tugs which were hastily assembled for a possible invasion were totally unsuitable for the task of crossing the Channel. Their average speed was about two knots and anything less than 12 knots would make them virtually sitting targets. Added to that was the fact that they were extremely unstable in choppy water and if there was one factor which could be relied on in the autumn it was that the Channel, which is otherwise unpredictable, could produce at least some choppy water. A factor not to be discounted entirely was that the barges were not specially built for invasion but had been removed from their normal industrial use; as long as the invasion plans were on, their absence would hamper German industry and, if they were sunk in an abortive invasion attempt, their loss could be an economic disaster.

Nevertheless the invasion project was approved in the renowned Directive 16 which was issued towards the end of July. The provisions of the directive were somewhat vague and optimistic in that it decreed that the RAF must be weakened to the point of being unable to put up effective resistance, the sea lanes to the landing beaches must be cleared of mines and British warships should be pinned down elsewhere. The landing must be a surprise and the first wave would take place between Ramsgate and the Isle of Wight. Subsequent landings would be made further north and further west. The invasion fleet would be protected on each flank from interference by the British Navy by the laying of broad banks of minefields. After much argument about the most suitable date and time, which could only be resolved by reference to tides, moonlight and weather forecasting, it was decided that the period between 19th and 26th September was the only one possible. Had the ghost of William the Conqueror been there to observe the drafting of Directive 16, he might have had a few cynical observations to make about predictions on cross-Channel invasion. An interesting provision was that the Luftwaffe should not destroy the harbours in southern Britain as these would be needed for unloading heavier materials later; the fact that the harbours would have been filled with mines if there was any danger of them falling into enemy hands did not seem to have occurred to the drafters of Directive 16.

The first requirement of destroying the RAF and the airfields proved to be easier to demand than to do. At the beginning of August the Luftwaffe set out to destroy the aircraft of Fighter Command in the course of an all-out offensive against south-east England. By mid-August it was realized that the Spitfires and Hurricanes and the control system were more than a match for whatever the Luftwaffe could launch against them, and the German losses were rapidly becoming unacceptable. What was not appreciated was the efficiency of British radar which showed the direction of the incoming planes and enabled adequate forces to be ranged against them. The impression was created that Britain had many more fighters than had been thought, and more, of course, than she possessed. The fact that Ultra was picking up Luftwaffe chatter was also an enormous help. In consequence, by mid-August the Luftwaffe abandoned its attempts to destroy aircraft in the air and instead settled for destroying the airfields they flew from, and if possible catching them on the ground. This proved far more effective than the previous policy and by early September it was realized that the RAF was now losing more fighters and pilots than it could replace at current rates of training and production.

Meanwhile, reports from air reconnaissance and information from agents revealed that the Germans now had enough barges to move at least 60,000 men. Guns for long-distance bombardment were being concentrated around Calais and the Luftwaffe was bringing dive bombers to the airfields close behind the Channel ports. Embarkation and disembarkation were being practised. Needless to say these preparations were being given full attention by Bomber Command and the persistent rumour that burnt German corpses had been washed up on the beaches of south-east England was probably true, but they did not come from an abortive invasion. In all probability they came from aircraft or barges which had been investigated by the RAF. The 'burnt corpses' story had been the subject of much speculation, and Churchill is said to have confirmed it. It has been suggested that if German corpses had been washed ashore the Red Cross would have been notified and their burial places recorded. This is undoubtedly true if they carried some form of identification. No identification, no record. Numerous unidentified corpses were buried after air raids and a few from the sea would have made little difference.

The 7th September was thought to be the most likely date. In fact a false alarm using the codeword 'Cromwell' was given on that day. It seems to have been based on the reported sighting of barges in the Channel. The church bells were rung, and it was nearly as difficult to stop them as it had been to start them. A more genuine invasion came from the air. Soon after five p.m. a wave of 320 bombers, escorted by 600 fighters, flew up the Thames and bombed every target they could find as far as Westminster. At eight o'clock another, smaller, wave (250) came in. Smaller flights appeared during the night to keep the fires stoked. Civilian casualties mounted to 7,000. But while the attacks on the capital built up, Churchill and the British Chiefs of Staff realized, almost incredulously, that the Germans had abandoned the policy which would have made invasion possible — i.e. the destruction of Fighter Command and the airfields — and instead were producing terrifying but militarily unimportant raids on London. This change of emphasis has never been explained. Perhaps Hitler felt that if London itself was subjected to terror raids the British public would demand that Churchill should sue for peace. It was not an unreasonable assumption for a person who was already misjudging the willpower of the British people. In London 12,696 were killed in three months of what became known as the Blitz (adapted from the German *Blitzkrieg* meaning 'lightning war'), and there were numerous casualties elsewhere, notably in Coventry but in many other industrial towns. Although the volume of air attacks lessened after 1940 they continued throughout the war and few were the places which did not hear the grinding roar of the German engines (de-synchronized to baffle anti-aircraft location) and the thump and crash of high explosive. There is nothing funny about the casualty rate running at about 5,000 a month but there was no shortage of jokes, such as those in bombed East End shops: 'Open as usual — even more so', or 'Business as usual during Altercations'. It was a curious time, in some ways slightly unreal. People who had originally rushed for shelter when the first air raid sirens sounded, now strolled around often unable to remember whether the warning or the all-clear was the last signal. Inhabitants of the Medway towns would take their lunch-time sandwiches to the park and eat them while gazing upwards at the life and death struggles between Spitfires and Messerschmitts being fought out in the sky crossed with trails of vapour and smoke. Everyone was only too well aware just how much national safety depended on a few young men fighting like old time champions in front of the assembled armies. Dover, not surprisingly, was given the nickname 'Hellfire Corner'; it had had similar experiences before but that did not make the 1940 one any the more palatable. On the 14th September Hitler decreed that an invasion should take place on the 17th and, to soften up the target, launched the biggest daylight attacks of the war on the 15th. Wave after wave came in and as they appeared on the radar screens the RAF hurled themselves against them. Losses on both sides were immediately reported, although inevitably they became somewhat exaggerated. Newspaper sellers had posters giving the casualties as cricket scores: 'Germany 68 for 19'. Eventually when the last German bomber disappeared from the horizon the score read Germany 185 all out. In fact the figures were much less. The final score for 15th September was 56 German aircraft down for the loss of 26 of our own. But it was enough. The Luftwaffe had failed to establish the necessary air superiority and the invasion date of 17th September was once again postponed. But the raids went on, although on a lesser scale. The invasion barges which had already been reduced in numbers by Bomber Command's attentions were removed from the Channel area, but not dispersed. An invasion was still very much on the cards, all it needed was a better ratio of success in the RAF–Luftwaffe conflict, and the next favourable tide. The latter factor ensured the postponement until 19th October when visibility would be likely to be worse and thus favour the invaders. But October came and went with no invasion. It seems that Hitler felt he had bigger fish to fry in the shape of Russia, and to weaken himself in a costly and unnecessary invasion of Britain would be pointless. It was one of his greater miscalculations.

But it might have happened. The naval and air attitudes have already been described, it remains to consider the German army's arrangements and the problems they would have encountered.

The German army planned to use forty-one divisions in the invasion. Six would come from the Calais area to land between Ramsgate and Bexhill, four from Le Havre would land between Brighton and the Isle of Wight, and three would land in or near Lyme Regis. The initial landing would take in 90,000 men. Two airborne divisions would be used in the first assault. The first objective would be to reach a line stretching roughly from Ramsgate to Brighton but bulging forward to include Uckfield, Tentenden, Ashford and Canterbury.

The embarkation and transport of 90,000 men from areas as far apart as Rotterdam and Le Havre and their disembarkation on suitable beaches would have been no mean problem, quite apart from any interference by the Royal Navy and Royal Air Force. For the final countdown there were 155 transports, 1,722 barges, and 471 tugs. This motley flotilla was assigned the task of maintaining the formation needed to aim invasion spearheads on to specific beaches; two at Rye; two between Folkestone and Dungeness, two at Bexhill and Pevensey, three around Newhaven. They would bring in 250 tanks and, as they disembarked, the first of the two allotted parachute divisions (the 7th) would land at Lympne. In theory this armada totalled eleven divisions in suitable places, but in practice some of them might have found themselves landing on such inhospitable areas as Beachy Head or Dover. The second wave of invasion troops, which would come in at captured ports, would bring in Panzer divisions whose role was to thrust up towards the Midlands and north. By this manoeuvre England would be split in two and London isolated. At best the whole operation could be completed in thirty days but after that there would still be plenty of mopping up to do.

Even allowing for the hazards of the Channel, the invasion forces looked a formidable prospect. Against it was a useful collection of large-calibre guns which included twenty at Dover, four at Newhaven, and many smaller ones which were dotted along the coast. The majority of the larger were naval guns from World War I and, until the Royal Artillery could take over the task, were mostly manned by RN personnel.

At the beginning of July, just after the fall of France, the Commander-in-Chief, Home Forces, was General Sir Edmund Ironside, a man of great stature in every sense of the word. However, his assessment of the situation, surveying the condition of the troops recently evacuated from Dunkirk, and the paucity of weapons to re-equip them, led him to concentrate his best troops in an inner ring around Redhill, Sevenoaks

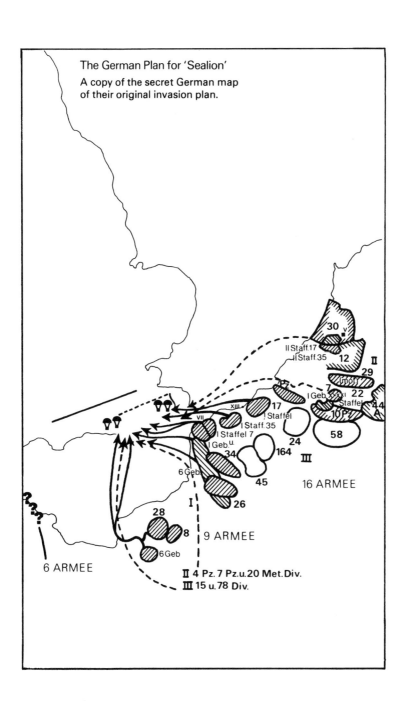

The German Plan for 'Sealion'

A copy of the secret German map of their original invasion plan.

30

II Staff. 17
II Staff. 35

12

II

29

7

I Geb.

XI

22

Staffel

44

A

17

I Geb.

XIII

I Staffel

10 P

7

VII

I Staff. 35

I Staffel 7

24

58

I Geb. u.

34

164

III

6 Geb.

45

16 ARMEE

I

26

28

8

9 ARMEE

6 Geb

6 ARMEE

II 4 Pz. 7 Pz. u. 20 Met. Div.
III 15 u. 78 Div.

and Maidstone up to the Thames estuary.

Not surprisingly this cautious, over-realistic view found little favour with those whose hearts were in Kent and Sussex, nor with Churchill. Accordingly, Ironside was replaced by General Sir Alan Brooke on 20th July. Alanbrooke, as he later became, reversed his predecessor's policy, and instead reinforced and re-equipped the troops in the forward areas. The expected landing points were all in the Kent and Sussex area, and thus were the responsibility of XII Corps under Lieutenant-General Andrew Thorne. Thorne had commanded a division in the retreat to Dunkirk and the Germans had already had reason to take note of his abilities. He set up his headquarters at Tunbridge Wells and allotted a specific, important task to every unit in his area. He was fully in favour of the Auxiliary Units and expected them to play a valuable part if called on. Coastal areas were cleared of all people not on essential work. In this area, as elsewhere, all signposts and place-names were removed so that any parachutist would have little idea of where he was or how to proceed to a useful objective. Removal of the signposts and station names probably caused far more confusion to the British than it would have done harm to the Germans. The two greatest reliefs as the war turned in our favour were the replacing of signposts and the easing of the blackout. Wars are nothing if not inconvenient. They are boring, expensive and at times dangerous; they are always maddeningly and frustratingly inconvenient.

Unfortunately Thorne's total strength only added up to four divisions, to which could be added Home Guard and other small units of unproved quality. At a pinch he could have two more divisions allotted to him, but these must move from another area. On paper it looks as if Thorne had an impossible task but the view was not shared by those in his command, even 45th Division which, deployed between Newhaven and Rye, had the task of holding one of the most vulnerable areas. When members of the 45th eventually learnt that no less than seven German divisions would have attempted to enter their area, they felt as flattered as they were relieved that Sealion had never been put into operation. Thorne commanded XII Corps until the following May when he was promoted to Scottish Command and his post taken by Lieutenant-General B.L.

Montgomery. But by then the Sealion plan had been abandoned.

Needless to say, the fact that the Germans had changed their
invasion plans and were now concentrating on Russia did not
in any way stop Britain preparing to repel whatever they
might produce in the future. Home Guard units maintained
their vigils, barbed wire was laid, sandbags were filled and
pillboxes constructed. By the time the Germans were well
embroiled in Russia and the Middle East, our state of readiness
was highly creditable.

One of the more interesting aspects of World War II is the
very multiplicity of projects which were in hand, mostly
secretly. Of Ultra and Double Cross we have already spoken
and there was, of course, the Special Operations Executive
working with our Allies in occupied countries. There were
scientists and engineers exploring everything from time-
bombs to directional beams, and there were experts in propaganda, deception and subterfuge. Very unmilitary-looking
inventors produced some valuable military equipment, such
as flails for anti-tank mines. The list seems endless but one of
the most interesting items on it was the use of flame.

Flame, as we know, had been used in warfare for over two
thousand years and the best kept secret was that of Greek fire.
According to Gibbon it was employed with equal effect on sea
or land, in battle or siege; it was most commonly blown
through tubes of copper that seemed to vomit a stream of
liquid and consuming fire. It was nourished and quickened by
the element of water; and sand, wine and vinegar were the
only remedies that could damp the fury of this powerful agent!

The possibilities of rediscovering this diabolical weapon
and using it as an anti-invasion measure interested a number of
leading politicians and led to the creation of the Petroleum
Warfare Department in July 1940. The old recipe never was
discovered but the use of flame-throwers subsequently owed
much to the experiments of this department. The first experiments were with flame traps which were placed by those
sunken roads which were deemed of sufficient importance.
Two hundred were installed. The method was to line the road
with perforated pipes which had been connected to a petrol
tank. On the approach of the enemy a tap would be turned, the

pipes flooded, and hell let loose by throwing some form of fireball into the middle of the petrol lake. When tried in practice it was impressive but dangerous even to the tap turner. The pipes were so well camouflaged that people going about their daily business rarely noticed them.

A development from flame traps was Fougasses. These were 40-gallon oil drums which were buried with a propellant charge at the lower end. When ignited — by remote control— they produced a thirty-yard spear of flame which demolished anything in its way. Some 40,000 of these were established in southern England and when General Thorne went to Scotland he introduced large numbers there.

The next stage was to see if the sea and beach could be set on fire. Some success was obtained by installing pipes which shot out petroleum over the beaches on to the sea. These were not too successful when the water was rough, but devastatingly effective when it was calm. Some of the experiments were observed by enemy aircraft, so in retaliation we dropped a series of leaflets on the Continent which were entitled 'Guide to Invasion' (in French, German and Dutch). They contained useful questions such as:

1. Do you think we shall ever get to England?
2. Why is the Führer not coming with us?
3. What is the charge for swimming lessons?
4. What is setting the sea on fire?
5. Does not the Captain burn beautifully?
6. Karl – Willi – Fritz – Johann is incinerated – drowned – chopped up by the propellers?
7. When is the next invasion due to take place?

The 'Little Manual of Conversation' was produced in September 1940 and dropped in millions. Britain may have been on the defensive but it was the defensiveness of the good-humoured bulldog at bay.

The flame-thrower scientists went on to experiment with mobile machines for tanks and these were used with great success in the later invasion of Germany. Few weapons are more terrifying and appalling than the modern flame-thrower, but its predecessors were doubtless feared as much in their day.

13 The Future — or not?

In 1979 the British people became uneasily aware that war as a means of policy had not become outmoded and that certain countries of the modern world were perfectly prepared to use war as a means of securing an objective or even of proving a point. In 1979 Vietnam invaded Cambodia in order to secure control of the Communist government there; shortly afterwards China invaded Vietnam to express displeasure at Vietnam's activities in Cambodia and also to warn the Vietnamese about encroaching on Chinese territory. The government of Angola had been established by Cuban and Russian help and it was clear that Clausewitz's dictum that war was the continuation of policy by other means had a number of advocates. Since World War II had ended there had been numerous conflicts in different parts of the world, some potentially very dangerous, and in Korea and in the Middle East. But whenever any war broke out, for whatever reason and in whatever part of the world, the principal interest was whether it would escalate. 'Escalate' is the modern term for spreading. If a war spread, larger and more vicious weapons would be used. As the 1970s came to an end there was a frightening realization that several countries now possessed weapons of enormous destructive power, e.g. nuclear weapons. Britain, France, Russia, America, China and India were already known to possess such weapons and it was already widely suspected that Israel and South Africa might have them too. There was a distinct possibility that other countries might shortly possess them, even if they did not already.

Because of the vast destructive power of nuclear weapons, a

new concept of warfare came into being. World War II had shown that even in life-and-death struggles certain weapons will not be used if both sides consider that the consequences would be unpredictable and make victory totally barren. One of these was gas, of which plentiful supplies were available, another, we suspect, was chemical agents. After World War II chemicals were occasionally used to defoliate jungle and to destroy crops in terrorists' camps, but they were not used against human beings. Limitation of method has been accepted and 'limited war' has come to mean wars limited to certain geographical areas and limited also in the type of weapon used.

Limited warfare was clearly a tremendous step towards a more sensible and, ultimately, peaceful world. It was conceived in an atmosphere of some psychological complexity. In spite of the fact that America and Russia had been allies in World War II, and America had supplied vast quantities of materials to its ally, it was clear throughout the war and after that Russia regarded the West with wary hostility. Russia had suffered the greatest losses of any combatant in World War II, with fifty-five million dead. She had been invaded by Germany, an eventuality she had aimed to prevent by allying herself with Germany in 1939; this move had given tacit approval to Hitler's rampages in the West. Stalin's paranoiac suspicion of anything emanating from the West caused him to disbelieve all the warnings he was sent about the imminence of that invasion, and the result was that Russia suffered far more than she needed. At the end of the war Russian armies had overrun several countries of eastern Europe and half Germany. From these she resolutely refused to budge and behaved as if she really believed that a Western country might still attack her and overthrow the Communist government. The 'Iron Curtain' came down across Europe and it was clear that the Russian government believed in offensive defence, that is, to edge the boundaries of her empire outwards and firmly crush any independence within. The policy was not successful with Yugoslavia which established independence though still remaining Communist.

The Western reaction was to create NATO, which incorporated West Germany. Contrary to post-war agreements,

Russia had already begun to rearm East Germany, with an army in the guise of a police force. For long it was believed that America's refusal to share the secret of the atomic bomb was the cause of Russian hostility, but long after Russia had her own bombs the same attitude prevailed. However, even when Russia was armed to the teeth with nuclear weapons she showed interest in agreements not to use them, and even more in agreements to prevent their use by countries which had recently acquired such weapons of mass destruction. At the same time she was in no way inhibited from stirring up trouble in any country outside her own empire, hoping to profit from the ensuing chaos and hoping that at the least the West would be weakened by the upheaval. And when other countries would have preferred to reduce their defence budgets they were prevented from doing so by the knowledge that Russia was increasing hers and already had an overwhelming collection of armaments of every sort, including a huge and powerful navy. At the same time Russia's economy was in a far from healthy state. Wheat to feed her population was imported from the United States (after fifty years of collective farming in some of the finest land in the world, the Steppes); Western technology had been freely bestowed on her, enabling her to develop weapons of infinite complexity and power. Various efforts were made to persuade Russia to agree to arms limitation and to be less oppressive to her dissidents. There was a reluctance to face the fact that Russia, although contantly using the word 'democracy', was as autocratic as she had been in the days of the Tsars, and that the attitude of hostility and suspicion to all countries not under direct Russian supervision — and even to some which were — had not changed significantly and was not likely to.

However, there had been progress. The installation of 'hot lines' between Moscow and certain other countries was designed to prevent the launching of nuclear war by accident. But the question which puzzled Western statesmen and strategists was — what were Russia's real intentions? Did they see world politics as a gigantic game of chess, a game at which their skill was legendary. It seemed probable that they did.

On this basis the prospects for peace did not seem too bad. The Russians would continue to pile up arms of every sort, back every form of subversion that they could turn to advantage, wrest what political concessions they might, saturate other countries with spies, and rule their own people and their satellites with an iron grip. The West might be beguiled into lowering its own arms strength, or might do it unilaterally as a gesture, however futile, as it has several times done; perhaps time alone could cause the bonds of NATO to disintegrate. One country after another would fall out, faced with massive Russian strength, even the once mighty America might merely protest feebly as the Russian bear ignored the bounds of diplomacy, decency and legality. All would be well, provided events were to the liking of the Russian leaders.

But two possibilities might be reckoned with. One was that there could be a mistake. A resistance movement could suddenly occur in a satellite country and prove more intractable than the one in Hungary in 1956 which had been promptly crushed with tanks. The second was that instability inside Russia itself could cause the Kremlin to make a hasty move destined to divert attention. That move might, for example, be concerned with Berlin, or the Middle East, or the West Indies. It was not a very likely possibility, for though the Russians could happily engage in trouble-fomenting in those or other areas, they would not normally wish to push their challenge to flash point.

But, unwittingly, they might. Once the real conflict started it would rapidly transfer to Europe. What would happen then is well into the realms of higher speculation for no one knows what court cards either side has up its sleeves. But fighting the war, on conventional terms, with known assets, it seems would favour Russia. At a war game played in connection with the television programme of *Invasion Road*, which was staged at the Royal United Services Institute, the 'Commander-in-Chief of NATO', Brigadier Peter Young, DSO, MC, MA, eventually found that, in spite of impressive victories in the north, he had run out of troops in the central sector. At that point NATO would have had to decide whether to be forced back or to use tactical nuclear weapons. Presumably that was NATO's last card. In fact it was not.

War games are a fascinating activity and are widely used, both as guides to policy and for harmless entertainment. Most of the military manoeuvres of recent years have been played out as war games, before and after the event. A war game was staged at the Staff College, Camberley, in 1973 on 'Sealion'. The competing teams were drawn from Germany and from the Royal Military Academy Sandhurst, and it was assisted by the *Daily Telegraph*. The findings were that Sealion would have failed. However it would be a considerable error to suppose that the occasion proved anything, for it was merely an entertaining unofficial exercise played by enthusiasts who in 1940 had no special knowledge of events, some in fact being children at the time. It certainly did not represent the concentrated wisdom and knowledge of Sandhurst and the Staff College. Likewise the RUSI war game was for entertainment rather than military enlightenment, although it paraded some distinguished and experienced warriors.

However, the ugly phrase 'The Third World War' began to be spoken rather than whispered in the late 1970s and the most knowledgeable assessment of it came from General Sir John Hackett, who published a book of that name and dated his conflict August 1985. In his imaginary war nuclear weapons were used but the war ended in three weeks with a victory for NATO. Although some of the data in the book will probably be made obsolete as we draw nearer to 1985, this book is likely to remain the classic on this subject.

But let us suppose that by a combination of supine behaviour and treachery in the West the Russians were enabled to reach the Channel ports. Let us further suppose that, having reached those ports, they could produce invasion fleets which, setting out from bases ranging from Germany to Le Havre, could land in Britain — without being atomized en route — what would be their prospects?

There would be several possibilities, all of which could conceivably occur at once. If the war had been nuclear from the beginning, large parts of the world, including much of Russia, would have become uninhabitable for generations. The Russian civilians who had avoided death in the war would emerge from their shelters to die of starvation and disease in the peace. Europe would have fared better, for if the Russian object was to conquer Europe they would hardly wish to destroy it before sending their armies into it; furthermore to destroy Europe would be to remove all possible prospect of gain from the war.

Thence to the second possibility. Since 1945 Russia has retained an iron grip on Czechoslovakia, Hungary, Poland and East Germany. Once the Russian armies moved to commitments elsewhere any of those countries, but particularly East Germany, would state their terms. Poland and East Germany are on the line of communication between Russia and Europe. Once the Russian armies had crossed into Europe there would be little to stop the East Germans and Poles moving the other way. Moscow itself could be threatened.

There are other intriguing possibilities. The Warsaw Pact countries have an impressive tank force, in fact, 60,000. The thought of this number of tanks, not to mention self-propelled guns and mobile rockets, moving on to the communications of Europe is a daunting one. Undoubtedly some would come well forward, but not perhaps 60,000.

But even if everything went like clockwork — the tanks did not embroil themselves in traffic jams, the satellite nations did not take the opportunity to rebel, the Chinese did not walk in through the back door, and the Russian people did not display undue unrest — there would still be one factor which would make the invasion of Germany, France and Britain a hazard of unpredictable consequences for Russia.

At present the Warsaw Pact armies are under control. There are two and a half million soldiers, with another five million in reserve (NATO matches this). The Warsaw Pact armies are well equipped, both in quantity of weapons and also in quality. But the very worst that could happen to them from the Russian point of view would be that they should be successful. For if they were, they would at once slip out of Russian control. In all probability after the first success the Warsaw Pact armies would disintegrate. A parallel might be found in the German troops who drove the Allies back in World War I in the spring offensive of 1918. As they drove a wedge deep into the Allied lines they saw the quality of the equipment the Allies had hastily and carelessly discarded. They did not see it so much as valuable loot as a symbol of something which would ultimately bring them defeat.

Undoubtedly the Russians are very strong in their army,

their navy and their air force. Undoubtedly they will grow stronger in all of these, for that is where the emphasis is put in their unbalanced economy. By that strength they can threaten, blandish, cajole, use instruments like the Cubans and East Germans to do their work for them. Through their extensive organization for spying and subversion they can do much to undermine and destroy the will to resist of other powers. But what, in the foreseeable future, they cannot do, is invade any country but those closest at hand, and even then with caution. For a Russian soldier outside the boundaries which the Kremlin has erected around him is no longer a docile Russian but a potential dissident. And the Russians have enough experience of dissidents not to wish to create two and a half million of them.

If the Russians opened their frontiers, tore down the Berlin Wall, and allowed free travel in and out of Russia and the satellite countries, it is possible, though unlikely, that the Russian people would feel that war for Kremlin policy was justified. But even if that happened, and in a non-nuclear war the Russians were able to extend their power over the rest of the Western world, including America, Africa and the Middle East, at what point would they find that they had passed the point of control? William I was able to conquer and subdue Britain in 1066 because he was dealing with a comparatively small area, but even he had troubles from the outlying districts, and some he never ventured into at all. Napoleon, in the early nineteenth century, sent his armies over Europe but was constantly having to fight his battles again. In the end, because he had so often overstretched himself, he tasted defeat.

The problems of invaders have been the subject of this book, and in conclusion it may be suggested that few activities are as hazardous. At best war is a ridiculous folly but when it includes invasion it takes risks beyond reasonable acceptability.

The Russians probably produce the best ballet dancers and chess players in the world. Their policy makers seem as light on their feet as their dancers; and they are always ready to sacrifice a pawn or two but never to risk a castle.

14 *A Matter of Self-Help*

However, the fact that success by Russian armies in a major war would lead to catastrophe, and the disintegration of the Russian state, gives no grounds for complacency in either West or East. The re-establishment of public services, of law and order, of agricultural and industrial production, would take months, perhaps years. The situation in Europe, and Britain, would be similar to that in the Thirty Years War of 1618–48 when, for the purest religious reasons, much of central Europe was turned into a waste over which wolves roamed. More than half the population, and in some towns four-fifths of the citizens, died. Modern sophisticated weapons would undoubtedly take their toll in a future war but the worst effects would probably come afterwards from the destruction of food, fuel and communications. In 1648 the survivors could gather a few sticks and make a fire, perhaps snare a rabbit; there would be little scope for that in Brussels, Paris, London or other modern cities.

Armed Russian soldiers, answerable to no one, would roam freely. It is interesting to reflect that in the 1980s most of the population of Britain knows less about the handling of weapons than guerrillas in undeveloped countries do. Rounding up and disarming freebooting Russian deserters would be a necessary first step but how and by whom it would be done cannot easily be envisaged.

At the moment the Russians seem to be organizing their plans for world conquest differently. Already they have a navy capable of challenging the West and at their present rate of building they are obviously intent on obtaining the same sort of numerical superiority that they have in tanks. Warsaw Pact missiles are so powerful and plentiful that the whole of Europe is at risk. And the Russians are still pressing on urgently with new ships, submarines, missiles, tanks and aircraft. Clearly their hope is that this overwhelming, even ridiculous, display of armaments will cause other nations to be frightened into accepting the expansion of Russian Communist influence. Undoubtedly the Kremlin would like to see pro-Russian governments in all the major countries of the world. It may seem unbelievably naive to think that Europe, North and South America, the Middle East, China and Japan could really be controlled by Moscow — or any one state — but that may well be the Russian dream.

But while that ambition of world domination lasts, the rest of the world, particularly Europe, should look searchingly at its future problems. In the 1930s Hitler gave ample warning of his intentions but few heeded him. In the 1970s the Russians have made it clear that their aim is to exploit any weakness of resolution in the West.

The lesson for those who do not wish to be invaded is that it is essential to be prepared for the worst. Those preparations need to extend to the period after a possible conflict. Any form of invasion is a major gamble for, whether military or political, it places unprecedented strains on the aggressor's resources. Those nations in the path of the invader must make clear by their own resolution and organization that the gamble is simply not worth the risk. It may be inconvenient and expensive and absurdly uncivilized to have to make such preparations but this is a matter in which there is no choice. We may not be able to stop the Third World War and we may not be able to contain it but we can make absolutely sure that we do not lose the peace which must eventually follow. And if we are able to win the peace there is a very reasonable chance that there will be no war.

Appendix A: Horsetroops

Writing in his book *The British Army* (Cassell, Petter and Galpin, 1865) Sir Sibbald Scott gives interesting information about 'hobby horses' which were used to carry invasion or raid warnings:

There was another class of horse-troops, of early institution, called Hobilers, who derived their designation from the small horses or 'hobbies' which they rode. It is uncertain when they were first organized, but frequent mention is made of them in the statutes of the fourteenth century and upwards. From their light equipment they must have been useful and necessary attendants on armies, the bulk of which was composed of knights and men-at-arms, armed cap-à-pie, who were incapable of practical duties where rapidity was required. Their horses are sometimes mentioned as 'equi dis-cooperti' as opposed to 'equi coopeati'. They acted as a corps of vedettes, and one of their most important functions was to carry information on the approach of an enemy. They were the channels of communication by day, as the beacons were by night. 'In old times,' says Camden, 'there were set horsemen at parts, in many places, whom our ancestors called hobelers, who in the day should give notice of the enemies' approach.' (*Britannia*, p. 196, edit. 1609). An old author, Minsheu (*Ductor in Linguas*, London, 1607), gives a further account of them: 'Hoblers, Hobellarii, are certain men, that by their tenure are tied to maintaine a little light nagge for the certifying of any invasion made by enemies, or such like perell towards the sea side, as Porchmouth, &c. Of these you shall reade an. 18 Edw. III., stat. 2, cap. 7, and an. xxv., ejusdem, stat. 5, cap. 8, and commeth of the French word Hobér, an old word, which is to move to and fro, to be stirring up and downe.'

For these purposes the hoblers would, doubtless, be selected from the residents on the sea-coasts, or the borders, and probably belonged to that class of small proprietors, who, possessing £15 in land, or goods to the value of 48 marks, were bound to provide for the service of the State 'a hauberk, sword, knife, and a horse'. As they were required for light and active duties, instead of the powerful war-horse, they were allowed to find any sort of horses, except mares.

Appendix B: Arrows

Sir Sibbald Scott records the following information:

Arrows were reckoned by sheaves, a sheaf consisted of twenty-four arrows. They were carried in a quiver slung on the right side, or at the back; those for immediate use were often worn under the girdle. The heads of arrows were of iron by statute 7th Hen IV. (1405–6), to be well boiled, brazed, hardened at the points with steel (*acerata,*) and marked with the maker's name.

The ordinary length of an arrow was half the length of the bow; and by 5 Edw. IV. (Irish Statutes) every Englishman and Irishman dwelling in England is obliged to have 'a bow in his house of his own length'. The 'cloth-yard shaft' was a frequent designation for an arrow; in Drayton's *Polyolbion* we read:

> They not an arrow drew,
> But was a cloth-yard long.

Some of the poetical legends extend it to a cloth ell.

Lord Verulam, in his history of Henry VII, p. 96, speaking of the encounter of the King's troops with the Cornish rebels at Blackheath, says: 'Most of them (the soldiers) were shot by arrows, which were reported to be of the length of a tailor's yard; so strong and mighty a bow the Cornish men were said to draw.'

Arrows, besides their ordinary usage, were sometimes employed as vehicles of combustible matter, to set on fire the enemy's works or shipping. On these occasions phials of

quick-lime, or of other inflammable substance, were fixed
on their heads and discharged from bows; and this was
practised long after the use of gunpowder. Strutt, in his
Horda (vol, i, pl, xxi.), has furnished an example of this
missile, from a MS of Matthew Paris, in Benet College,
Cambridge, and in the Additamenta to the printed history
of Matthew Paris, it is recorded that at the capture of
Damietta, 'we discharged fiery darts (*spicula ignita*) at them;'
further on, 'phials full of lime (*phialas plenas calce)* were
discharged against the enemy, like little darts from bows'.
Neade says he has known by experience that an archer may
shoot an ounce of firework upon an arrow twelve score
yards. At the siege of Harfleur, it is narrated that raging fire
was hurled against the French. An author publishes in the
seventeenth century what he is pleased to term *A New
Invention of Shooting Fire-shafts in Long-bows.* (Lond. 1628).
In order to test their efficacy, he recommends 'that at festival
times a bull (instead of baiting him with dogs) were tied to a
stake, or sheweld in with archers, conveniently placed upon
a common or other spacious place, men might then make
trial with their fire-shafts (a brave and warlike sport), where
happily the madding of the enraged beast, besides inuring
men to conflict, would teach some profitable stratagem for
war.'

His plan is to insert 'a pipe of latten' in the end of the
arrow, and to have it filled with a mixture of gunpowder
and saltpetre, and a small quantity of camphor. The charge
is to be lighted, and to be shot in the ordinary way from the
bow. Grose says, 'arrows with wild-fire, and arrows for
fireworks, are mentioned among the stores at Newhaven
and Berwick, in the first of Edward VI.'

In Psalm cxx, we find the 'sharp arrows of the mighty,
with coals of juniper', which may point to a practice of using
arrows with some burning material attached to them. Sir
John Hawkins, in his *Voyage into the South Sea in 1593*
(re-published by Hakluyt Society, 1847), records the use of
fire-arrows for damaging an enemy's rigging: 'to teare of
spoile his tackling and sayles, billets of some heavy wood,
fitted to the great ordinance, are of great importance; and so
are arrows of fire, to bee shott out of slur-bowes'.

There are some remarkable specimens of fire-arrows in the Rotunda, Woolwich.

The distance at which an arrow can be shot from a longbow, with the best elevation of forty-five degrees, depends upon the strength and skill of the archer. It ranges from ten to twenty score yards. The exploit of one man, who shot a mile in three flights, is recorded as something very extraordinary. Shallow, in speaking of 'a fine shot' *(2 Hen. IV., iii.2)* — 'he would have clapped i' the clout at twelve score, and carried you a forehand shaft a fourteen and fourteen and a half, that it would have done a man's heart good to see' — evidently mentioned this distance as a feat achieved. By the 33rd Hen. VIII., no one who had attained the age of twenty-four might shoot at any mark at less than 220 yards' (eleven score) distance under a penalty of 6s 8d for each shot. In a MS of the 'Archers' Marks in Finsbury Fields', in the possession of the Society of Antiquaries, the greatest majority of distances recorded are between ten and nineteen score yards, there being but one of twenty and three of twenty-one score mentioned.

According to Neade, the range of a long-bow was from sixteen to twenty score yards, and so quick were the archers or so slow the musketeers, that six arrows could be discharged in the time that a musket could be loaded and fired once. This fact, however, will tend to remove any surprise that archery should have continued in force so long after the invention of gunpowder.

It is curious to hear a British officer, at the end of the eighteenth century, recommending the re-introduction of bows and arrows; a fact which assures us of the miserable practice of musketry in those days. This will be found in the *Memoirs of the Life of the late Charles Lee, Esq.,* Lieutenant-Colonel of the 44th Regiment, Colonel in the Portuguese Service, &c. (1792).

'I still wish', he writes, 'that pikes could be introduced, and I would add bows and arrows

'1. Because a man may shoot as truly with a bow as with a common musquet.

'2. He can discharge four arrows in the time of charging and discharging one bullet.

'3. His object is not taken from his view by the smoke of his own side.
'4. A flight of arrows coming upon them, terrifies and disturbs the enemies' attention to his business.
'5. An arrow sticking in any part of a man, puts him hors de combat till it is extricated.
'6. Bows and arrows are more easily provided anywhere than musquets and ammunition.'

The practice of archery was very much neglected even when the glory of the English archers was at its zenith, and Edward III commanded the sheriffs of London to see that the male population should recreate themselves on holidays with archery. The same command was repeated in the 12th Richard II. An act of Edward IV (1465–6) directs that butts should be erected in every township, at which the inhabitants were to shoot up and down, upon all feast days, under the penalty of one halfpenny for every time they omitted to perform this exercise. By the repeated entries in church-wardens' accounts for the expenses of erecting these, we may infer that they were erected in or adjacent to the churchyards in the country. It appears that they were made of turf. In London a large space was reserved for the practice of archery, and it has already been stated that Charles I issued a commission, in the eighth year of his reign, to prevent the fields near London being so enclosed as to prevent the necessary and profitable exercise of shooting, and also to lower the mounds where they prevented the view from one mark to another.

As an encouragement to archers, it was laid down by an act of Henry I, c.88, that if any one in practising with arrows, or with darts, should by accident kill another, it was not to be visited against him as a crime. The same immunity was confirmed in after years by Henry VIII, who, amongst other privileges granted by him in the twenty-ninth year of his reign to the Artillery Company, decreed that if any person passing between the shooter and the mark be killed, it shall not be murder, provided the archers have first called out 'Fast' (meaning, of course, 'Stand Fast').

That young archers might acquire an accurate eye, and a

strength of arm, none under twenty-four years of age might shoot at any standing mark, except it were a 'roaver', and then he was to change his mark at every shot, under the penalty of fourpence for any shot made contrary to this regulation.

Ascham informs us that the marks were termed 'butts, prickes, and roavers'. The 'butt' was a level mark, at a moderate distance; the 'pricke' was a 'mark of compass', but certain in its distance; while the 'roaver' was a mark of uncertain distance. Edward VI, in his journal, says, 'I lost the challenge of shooting at rounds, and won at roavers'. The first we may understand as being shots at targets or any similar fixed objects, at a measured distance; the latter any objects, at uncertain distances, such as a tree, a gate, or any given field object that occurs. The term seems to be drawn from the roving of the shooters from one object to another. 'The Cornish men', says Carew, 'are well skilled in near shooting, and in well-aimed shooting; the butts made them perfect in the one, and the roaving in the other; for the prickes, the first corrupters of archery through too much preciseness, were formerly scarcely known, and little practised.'

Archery supplied the means of employment to a great number of hands. Bowyers, fletchers, string and arrowhead makers, were all so many different trades; and in order that distant counties might be furnished with these important artificers, if they were not freemen of the City of London, they were liable to be sent to reside in any part of the realm where their services might be deemed requisite, under a penalty of forty shillings for every day's neglect. For foreign garrisons in the time of Edward II, one artificer or armourer, styled 'artillator', was appointed.

Long-bows were protected from the weather in cases, a fact which may have materially influenced the success of the English at Crécy. Shakespeare alludes to this custom, in making Falstaff apply the term of 'a bow case' to 'Prince Hal' (I Henry IV., act ii, sc. 4). Bow-strings, according to Ascham, were usually made of hemp, others of flax or silk.

To have 'two strings to one's bow' was, as may be supposed, a very necessary precaution. 'If a string breaks the man is lost,' wrote Ascham; and a law of Charlemagne, issued AD 813, enjoins the double provision. 'Et ipse comes provideat quomodo sint parati, milites aut arcum cum duabus cordis.' *(Capit. Reg. Fr.,* a S. Baluzius, 509)

Appendix C: Surgery

Although there are a few graphic illustrations of surgery after every battle so little has been written on this subject that we must conclude that first aid for the wounded was sparse and rudimentary. However, it is likely that people who could have teeth drawn with pliers and whose only anaesthetic was strong drink were much less sensitive to pain than modern man.

Sir Sibbald Scott has this to say of early surgery:

> Military surgeons are seldom mentioned in the records of our ancient armies. The disproportion between the troops employed and the persons engaged to attend to the injuries they received in action is very remarkable. The fact was, that the poorer soldiers, when seriously wounded, were discharged with a small gratuity to find their way home as best they might: a practice founded on the economical principle, which prevailed as late as the sixteenth century, that 'it cost more to cure a soldier than levy a recruit'. When, however, we consider the low state of the healing art, and the painful remedies applied (a medical writer of the sixteenth century recommends for the 'curation' of gun-shot wounds, 'to cauterize them with the oil of elders, mixed with a little treacle'), it is pretty certain that this, under the circumstances, was also the most humane course to be pursued. Nor can we wonder at the contempt with which surgery was held in this island down to the beginning of the sixteenth century, when it was practised indiscriminately by barbers and farriers.

> The position of a soldier in the event of a dangerous

wound must have been dreadful, and thousands doubtless died from bad surgery, or no surgery at all, especially when we find that ' a famous chirurgion at Turin' proposed such a panacea as the following as a balm for gunshot wounds: 'Two young whelps, one pound of earth worms, two pounds of the oil of lilies, six ounces of the terebinth of Venice, and one ounce of aqua vitae; in my presence he boiled the whelps alive in the said oil, until the flesh deserted from the bones; afterwards he took the worms, having before killed and purified them in white wine, to purge themselves of the earth, which they have always in their bodies. Being so prepared, he boiled them also in the said oil, till they became dry; this he strained thorow a napkin, without any great expression; that done he added thereto the terebinth, and lastly the aqua vitae, and called God to witnesse that this was his balme, which he used in all wounds made by gunshott and in others which required suppuration; withall praying me not to divulge his secret.'

Appendix D: Napoleon's Invasion Fleet

Fifty-four *prames* in two divisions were to form a *flottille de grande espèce*. Each boat was capable of carrying three officers, twenty-five infantry, fifty cavalry, and two non-combatants, making a total of eighty men. The cargo would consist of a formidable array of munitions of war: twenty-seven muskets, twenty bayonets, 200 tools, 12,000 cartridges, 1,200 rations of biscuit, 500 rations of oats and the same of bran, fifty horses, sixty saddles, and six sheep. In the fifty-four vessels 4,320 men were disposed of.

The flotilla of sloops was to remain at 324 vessels, as already planned, and each was to be accompanied by a small pinnacle. Three officers of a company, ninety-one officers and soldiers, two officers of the battalion staff, one officer of the general staff, three gunners, three waggoners, and eight surgeons, making a total of 111 men, was the complement of each *bateau*, or 35,964 in all. Twenty-seven muskets, twenty bayonets, twenty-seven pioneers' tools, 1,200 flints, 12,000 cartridges, 1,200 rations of biscuit, 150 pints of brandy, and four sheep were also to be stowed away in each sloop.

The gunboats, of which there were to be 432, were each to carry 130 men, making a total of 56,160 men, including 3,456 surgeons, formed a third flotilla. A piece of field artillery in addition to the 24-pounder with which they were armed was to be carried, and a cargo similar to a sloop, plus two horses, ten bushels each of oats and bran, and 200 rounds of shot. As in the case of the sloops, a pinnace was to go with each gunboat. A further 2,160 soldiers were to cross the Channel in 540 *caïques*, loaded with 216,000 cartridges, 21,600 rations of biscuit, 1,080 rations of brandy, and 108 sheep.

A fifth flotilla of eighty-one corvettes, each holding forty soldiers, added 3,240 men to the number already noted. These also carried the same kind of cargo as the *bateaux canonniers*, but without the artillery and ammunition. Fishing boats to the number of 108 were to transport 2,160 horses and riders, with a double supply of saddles and bridles. Biscuits, brandy, sheep, and fodder also found a place in the hold.

The figures quoted above can only convey a crude idea of the enormous amount of munitions of war it was necessary to carry to England. The transport flotilla was to be composed of six distinct classes of fishing vessels, 464 of which were calculated to carry no fewer than nearly three million cartridges and 1,208 horses, as well as food, guns, bridles, and the thousand and one things indispensable to a campaign. Canteen women to the number of 1,760, and 3,560 men and officers, in addition to the crews, were also to be accommodated. Moreover, from 100 to 150 large armed fishing vessels disposed of a further 200 horses, 1,000 men, 10,000 biscuits, and 1,000 rations of brandy, oats, and bran respectively, and 200 sheep. The army of invasion as then planned was to have a total strength of 114,554 men, including 76,798 infantry, 11,640 cavalry, 3,780 artillery men, 3,780 waggoners, and 17,467 non-combatants. It may be noticed that there were several thousand troops in excess of the number allowed for in the boats, but it was found that each vessel was able to accommodate from twelve to fourteen men in excess of their official complement.

(These figures are based on Desbrière, Vol. III, pp.98–105.)

Index